CHEESECAKE LOVES MY THIGHS

AND 27 OTHER REASONS WHY CHEESECAKE IS BETTER THAN MEN

Cheesecake Loves My Thighs

AND 27 OTHER REASONS WHY CHEESECAKE IS BETTER THAN MEN

MARIANNE SPRANGERS

MARIANNE SPRANGERS

ALSO WRITES BLOG POSTS

Cheesecake Is Better than Men
(www.cheesecakeisbetterthanmen.com)

and

Unforeseeably Single
(www.unforeseeablysingle.wordpress.com)

WWW.MARIANNESPRANGERS.COM

Paperback ISBN: 979-8-9866284-0-0
eBook ISBN: 979-8-9866284-1-7

Edited by Sasha Boyce and Debra Nichols
Cover design by Jay Cohen

This book is dedicated to the heating elements in my oven that went haywire long before the last recipe was tested.

Contents

PROLOGUE

It was my fourth or fifth year of college and not only had partying hard lost its appeal but threats of graduation and finding "a real job" took my joy and turned it into an almost panic level of fear. Graduation was both the bright, shiny light at the end of the tunnel I could finally see and the reality train that was about to flatten me like a penny on the tracks.

Tuition money wasn't spent wisely on my higher education, rather it was squandered on cheap wine, duct-tape car repairs, new guitars, and on the accidental education that comes with less-than-adult decisions. College was about growing up and despite the cost, I fought it with the vigor of a toddler at naptime. I still had so much to learn. Loans and grants put me in the classroom, but the real expenditure happened everywhere else. There was a return on this investment that eventually came one slice at a time in the form of a love that I had never known before.

Learning about love meant taking an entirely different set of tests for which the Cliff Notes of life had not prepared me well enough. Even though I read every page of *Tiger Beat* as an adolescent, every page of *Seventeen* as a teen, and took every quiz in my aunt's *Cosmo* mags, I still intertwined words of love and acts of sex, not understanding that these are two totally separate things. I confused arguments with endings; kindness with boring; and everything in between as frustration. Dating felt like taking a mythology exam with an abacus, a broken pencil, and a circus monkey for tutorial support.

Love, in the way that my grandmother described it, was a *knowing*. She knew when she met my grandfather in kindergarten, threatening him with the idea of marriage before she could even spell his last name. She knew at age five that he was her ever after. My attempts at similar portends usually ended up with a call to my mom and a plea to focus on my schoolwork.

Dating seemed like it should have been as simple as slide-on slippers. It was and remains anything but. It feels more like a knotted wad of laundry when I washed one pair of nylon stockings and a bra in one load with everything else. Instead of clean clothes, I'd created an oversized, fifteen-pound mass of wet fabric that took a winch, needle-nosed pliers, and three days to unravel. I'd love to say that it was worth the effort to sort through it all, but honestly, unless the bra worked the miracle of making A-cups into cleavage, it wasn't. This is how complicated and disappointing dating felt.

The unbalanced lump of laundry that I called my love life left me declaring war on dating and making an entire gender enemy number one. I had no idea what to do with this epic disenchantment, so I did what so many of us Soured Sallies do. First, I cried. Then I blamed myself, noted all my flaws and tried to change everything I could about myself with the hope of becoming more lovable, and eventually (and always), I turned to food.

I cooked. I baked. I stuffed, stirred, crammed, and jammed every unforgiving feeling into the wide-open crevasse where my tender heart used to be. Some foods were better than others at providing comfort and, surprise of all surprises, salad was not one of them. Comfort came with the stuff that sticks with you: sugar, fat, yum, and delicious. The biggest comfort, the one food that embodied contentment the most, and the one food in which the process of making and eating held the greatest meaning and provided the greatest pleasure, was cheesecake.

Cheesecake, like all good accessories, went with my many moods and emotionally driven haircuts and colors. It completed and complimented me the way ankle boots do to my ripped jeans and linen shirt.

As true allies do, the cheesecake just showed up one day and let me know in so many ways that it was going to stick with me. That's when I knew, as sure as my grandma did when she met my grandpa. So, like a general who recruits soldiers for battle, I gathered the broken-hearted and the disillusioned lovelorn friends for a march against men and for eternal validation that we were right, and they were wrong. If *hell hath no fury like a woman scorned*, then imagine a room full of us.

Every Monday night in what became the final year of undergrad, as if we needed more fuel in the pack of our verbal cannons, we girlfriends jacked ourselves up on coffee, wine, sugar, and the fatty goodness of cheesecake. The common ground of disappointment had been established. Dating felt like a losing battle. We drew the scrimmage lines, repeatedly. We placed blame with all fingers pointing outward and cracked jokes at everyone's expense but our own. We cried, laughed, and ate more cheesecake before making the logical leap to comparative values: *Cheesecake is rich,* we said. *Cheesecake is sweet. Cheesecake loves my thighs. The size of your cheesecake doesn't matter.* The list was endless, the laughter loud.

For the first time in my college career, I took notes.

The list, however, came to a screeching halt shortly after the mortarboards were tossed in the air. As fun as waging war had been, we all scrambled to find a sense of security outside of our useless degrees and within the comfort of companionship. None of us intentionally set out for an MRS degree but somehow, we all got one. The sky finally opened after graduation—the angels sang and filled the space with love where textbooks, junk food, and vindication desserts used to be. Happily ever after's, rings, vows, and fancy dresses had arrived for us all, including me.

Married life, for a few of us—okay—*one* of us, fell into the wah-wah-what-the-hell category of whoops-I-probably-should-have-thought-that-through. Back to the dating world I went.

All subsequent experience—in dating and baking alike—has left me a little worse for wear. I'm a smidge wiser, thumbing through my old cheesecake recipes with sweet nostalgia and reviewing a list that has held its own over the years. And, in reviewing that list, I've added to it.

OH, CHEESECAKE, MY CHEESECAKE

The myriad Cheesecake Factory restaurants that populate major corners of almost every mall today didn't exist when I was in college. Ponderosa, *"the place for steak,"* occupied those corners. Back then The Cheesecake Factory was one—ONE—small, family-owned restaurant in Beverly Hills that only folks in Beverly Hills knew about. Cheesecake was apparently only for the rich and famous.

The World Wide Web didn't exist at that time and Google was paired with eyes attached to yarn and glue crafts. It wasn't the verb it is today.

Nobody had heard of Rachel Ray, Martha Stewart, or Great Bake Off shows. Nor was there any Cake Boss outside of a five-year-old having a tantrum at a birthday party.

It was a different time and place where access to absolutely everything meant a trip to the library, the museum, or watching the original *Star Trek* with hopes that someday video-screen conferencing will be a real thing.

Food was no different.

There was little opportunity to step beyond "that's how my mother made it" meals and most desserts either came out of a box or you wished they did. Recipes were handed down on 3 × 5 index cards, neatly scripted with someone's mother's hand—the hand that left off key ingredients should a recipe ever stray from the family. God forbid anyone learn about the nutmeg in the banana bread.

My grandmother, Mary Anne Sprangers, who volunteered in the elementary school clinic in the mornings and bowled with a raucous bunch of solidly middle-class, coifed weekly, red-lipstick wearing, wild women in the afternoon, had a wooden recipe box filled with said 3 × 5 cards. Many had brown, missing edges from thumbing past and from occasional use, and even more were misfiled or had only one part of the recipe or another. She made excellent tuna casserole and baked macaroni and cheese, of which the index cards were useless to both her and the generation to whom she passed them down.

Her chili, also not inscribed on any index card, consisted of canned tomato soup, ground beef, spaghetti noodles, and—the key ingredient—chili powder. Without the powder, it was just soup. She also made potatoes from a box, green beans from a can, and breakfast was either cereal in a bowl or donuts from a bag.

Her desserts either involved canned fruit or had directions that fell along the lines of "just add water" on the boxes. Truth be told, though, she preferred boxes that came either from the bakery section of the grocery store or out of the freezer and left on the counter to thaw.

My grandmother had a few desserts in her repertoire that were akin to her chili: simple. She made mandarin orange cake with canned oranges or cheesecake. Grandma's cheesecake was not the kind of cheesecake that would inspire a young twenty-year-old college kid to set out on a mission that would take the next thirty years to fulfill. The quest I embarked upon, setting out to find that one perfect cheesecake recipe that would sound the siren of '*who needs men anyway,*' was not based on my grandmother's cheesecakes. Not even close.

One of her cheesecakes, you'll be shocked to learn, came from a box. She didn't make it often. The grandkids, who ate everything she popped out of a cardboard container, wouldn't touch it.

The other cheesecake contained Cool Whip and powdered sugar and was topped with canned cherry pie filling, which made it an instant success as a dessert, a key to attention deficit, a preparatory agent for races up and down the steps, and a consequent reason for parents to yell.

Its sugar content could cause blindness.

Regardless of her culinary laissez-faire attitude in the kitchen, her food, especially her cheesecake, came with a side order of wisdom. I absorbed the cheesecake. The acumen, however, was left like crumbs on the plate and washed down the sink with obedience but little foresight or understanding.

Grandma's cheesecake saw me through the divorce of my parents when I was young, and the alien abduction of my first love in elementary school. It was there for me through the almost completed alphabet of ex-boyfriends in high school, and again in college as I searched for the husband that I would later leave. It almost made it with me to the altar—but I had, at that time, found another cheesecake.

AH, LOVE

The first time I fell in love it was with Donny. He was new to our farm-fed school in second grade, and I spotted him the way my grandmother spotted my grandfather all those year ago.

The school itself could have easily been mistaken for a 1950s office building except for a basketball court and playground on one end of the brick box and a small graveyard on the other. These unrelated things used to be closer together, but the teachers wanted a parking lot. A field of wildflowers was eventually fenced in and paved over to accommodate this request.

It was the first day of school when the new kid was introduced to Mrs. Mack's second-grade class. On the first day of any school year, all the parents wrangled their freckled faced, cowlicked-hair offspring into Sunday clothes so we could make a good first impression on the teacher. Like so many, I, too, was squirming in discomfort. My mom made me wear a skirt. Always trying to keep up with my older brothers, I found skirts to be impractical. But there I was all dressed up for Mrs. Mack—or so I thought.

He was standing in front of the class like a beacon or a star. All shiny, tiny, and new.

When Donny was asked to find a partner to show him around the school, he scanned the room and chose "legs in the skirt." It was the seventies. Objectification wasn't in our vocabulary yet. Girls were taught that was flattery. It was so much a part of our vernacular that even Mrs. Mack let it slide and I was partnered with Donny for the remainder of the week.

I wore skirts through Friday and beyond. I even asked my mom to get me *nylons* so I could ditch the tights and clogs. Donny was one of the shorter kids in the class and I was one of the tallest. Wearing flats would reduce my height by one inch. I measured.

As the year progressed, we became inseparable. We shared a love for prepackaged snack cakes, pizza day, everything chocolate, and our teacher, vying for her attention as a team. Donny was my best friend. My eight-year-old heart had found its little twin flame and I was inspired beyond just fashion changes. I practiced my cursive, writing our names with swirls and arrows. I scrubbed my fingers with a brush and soap and applied polish to my nails. My mom made a lot of allowances for my adoring heart. I was allowed to talk to Donny for ten minutes on the phone after dinner. It was a blissful eternity. I was clear to let her know that this was not the puppy love of first grade. This was the real thing.

My brothers heckled me endlessly because of it.

At the end of third grade, still starry-eyed in my now two-year, long-term relationship with Donny, I learned a little more about love. We sat next to each other on field trips, stood next to each other in line and picked each other first for kickball. We were partners in everything. We were nine. I remember it like it was yesterday.

At the end of the summer between third grade and fourth, I biked my usual route to Donny's house. I pedaled through the subdivision where I lived, across a corn field, and over a country highway to the green, split-level ranch where Donny lived with his three older siblings, their parents, and what felt like an entire pack of wiry, tail-wagging dogs. The sky was end-of-summer-blue. The air was just beginning to hint that fall was on its way. The only care I had in the world was whether we would bike to the ice-cream stand or play in the backyard.

It was then that I saw the one thing my nine-year-old brain couldn't process. I saw the impossible. Donny's house was EMPTY. There was a "For Sale" sign in the front yard.

All my breath left my body. Everything became very still. Minutes felt like an eternity as I tried to take it all in.

The neighbor lady was tending to her yard. She was still there. The neighbors on the other side were still there. Donny's family wasn't. They were gone. There was no good-bye and no forwarding address.

Right there, on his front lawn with one leg as a kickstand and the other still on the pedal, I felt my heart shatter inside my body, and painful tears dripped from my eyes. My love abandoned me and was never seen again. Ever. Vanished. No words. No note. No good-bye or see you later. Just gone. Alien abduction for certain. I stared for a long time, trying to take in what was missing. There wasn't a bike in the yard or a flowerpot on the front porch. There wasn't a plastic floral wreath on the front door. There was no laundry on the line and even the laundry line itself was missing. Everything was missing: Donny, his bike, and the noise that belonged to his large family—all missing. In all the world, I could not have felt more alone. I felt duped. I felt hijacked. Surely this was a trick; a joke; a terrible, terrible prank. Slowly, I turned myself around at the off-the-reel announcements of the neighbor lady, "They're not there, Sweetie," letting the abandonment wash over me like ice-cold water as the Titanic of my love sank into an abyss and cried my nine-year-old eyes out all the way home.

And so began my love life.

THE DISAPPEARING ACT

(Chocolate Hazelnut Cheesecake)

INGREDIENTS:

Crust

- 1½ cups graham crackers
- 1 cup hazelnuts, toasted and cooled
- 2 T cocoa powder
- 2 T flour
- ⅓ cup sugar
- ½ cup butter

Cheesecake

- 3 (8 oz) packages cream cheese, room temperature
- ½ cup sugar
- ⅔ cup chocolate hazelnut spread
- 1 tsp vanilla extract
- 1 T instant espresso coffee
- ½ cup sour cream
- ⅓ cup heavy cream
- 2 eggs plus 2 egg yolks
- 4 (1 oz) semisweet chocolate baking squares, finely chopped into tiny pieces

Topping

- 4 (1 oz) semisweet chocolate baking squares, finely chopped
- Cinnamon
- ¼ cup heavy cream
- Hazelnuts, toasted and chopped fine

DIRECTIONS:

Preheat oven to 350° F. Grease the bottom and sides of a 9" springform pan. For crust, place crackers and nuts into a food processor and pulse until they are crumbs. Add sugar, flour, and cocoa powder. Pulse until blended. Transfer to a bowl and add butter. Combine until the mixture sticks together. Press the mixture into the bottom and sides of the springform pan. Bake for 8 minutes. Set aside to cool.

Wrap the cheesecake pan in a double layer of aluminum foil, and place in a large, deep baking pan to prepare for the water bath.

In a bowl, mix cream cheese and sugar until smooth. Add hazelnut spread. Mix. Add sour cream. Mix. Scrape down bowl often to ensure even mixing. Add espresso and heavy cream. Beat until smooth and creamy. Add eggs, one at a time, and mix until blended. Add vanilla extract. Mix. Stir in chocolate pieces. Pour over prepared crust and add 1" of water to the outer pan to create a water bath.

Bake for 50–60 minutes or until cheesecake is set on the edges but still jiggly in the middle. Turn off oven and let sit for 30 minutes. Remove from oven and cool to room temperature (about 2 hours).

Run a knife along the inside edge of the pan to release the cheesecake and prevent cracking.

To make topping, place cream in a small bowl and heat in a microwave until hot (about 20 seconds). Pour over chocolate pieces and let stand for 1 minute. Mix until smooth. If more heat is needed, place bowl over another bowl with hot water in it.

Pour over cheesecake. Garnish with hazelnuts. Refrigerate at least 4 hours or until ready to serve.

1.

YOU ARE SUPPOSED TO BITE
INTO CHEESECAKE

Jumping rope in second grade taught me pretty much everything I needed to know about relationships. First came love, then came marriage, then came a baby in the baby carriage. I never questioned it. When the rhyme asked, "How many kisses does she receive?" the twirl of the ropes and the tapping of white Keds on pavement sped up into a mad rush of numbers and sweat. I was hoping to get enough kisses to get to the good stuff, even though I had no idea what the good stuff really was.

This particular form of poetic exercise validated my grandmother's hard line that kissing got you pregnant. She must have jumped rope in elementary school, too.

My grandmother's warning sounded out in my head with staccato-like repetition and vim, which caused me anxiety in the fifth grade thanks to the occasional game of spin the bottle behind the school.

Fortunately for me, no baby-making seeds took hold on my lips, thanks in part, I'm certain, to the fruit-scented, apparently prophylactic magic of Bonnie Belle. I kept on kissing boys.

It wasn't long before locking lips became a thing of a different interest, moving from the frolic status of a spinning bottle to a finite and targeted effort. Feelings and crushes and jealousy and status and comparison all arrived within minutes of the bottle landing on one target or the other. "Like" went to "*like*-like." Scales of one through ten appeared on folded notes that were inconspicuously passed while a teacher wrote something about sentence structure on a green chalkboard.

I was learning about LOVE and kissing and blushing and being sneaky about it, and, at that time, *See Jane run* was still just a simple, meaningless sentence.

Right around the time I began mummy wrapping my chest in elastic and, later, underwire, I started getting picky about which boys I wanted to kiss. I also became particular about what I liked and didn't like in mouth-mashing efforts. Some boys I wanted to kiss but never had the opportunity. Others I wish I hadn't. There were good kissers, all lovely lips and sweetness, and then there weren't. Some were downright awful. You never forget the bad ones. Bad kissers fell into categories such as "Jaws," "Face Plant," "Moaner," "Tongue Jammer," "Licker," and the "Juicy Peach." We know who these kissers are. We also know that these kissers made it into adulthood using their mouth like that. Somewhere out there, though, they found their chompy, sloppy, slobbery match. It clearly wasn't me.

I remember the first time I was attacked by Jaws. My grandparents had a summer cottage on an inland lake. Every May through August, I had a completely different set of friends, hobbies, and bad habits than during the school year. The face mauling happened there sometime between "kissing gets you pregnant" and "do you have a condom?"

The lake was small and the number of kids my age was limited to a few. Lake life in Wisconsin has a finite number of days between the last bell of the school year and the first of the next. Between the time crunch and the scarcity of available adolescents, crushes were recycled amongst the group of hormonal adolescents and teens. It was my turn to crush on the neighbor boy. He was two years my senior, had a speedboat and freckles, and spent a lot of time making small talk with my grandparents.

Flirting and being pushed off the dock were synonymous. Being snapped with a towel was somehow flattery and having someone tip your canoe only meant one thing: some kissing was going to happen. My canoe got tipped.

In the air-pocket space of the overturned boat, legs bumping into each other with the wave of the water, the neighbor boy made his move. He moved his face toward mine as I closed my eyes, softened my lips, and moved my face toward his. *Little House on the Prairie* showed me how it was done when Almanzo kissed Laura. That's how I saw this going down. Unprepared, I felt his unexpectedly wide-open mouth cover the lower half of my face. His teeth landed on my cheeks, uppers firmly implanted on one side and lowers on the other. Stunned, my eyes popped open as I watched my own face being gnawed on by a boy I immediately no longer liked. My lips were still puckered inside of his unhinged jaw. To save myself from being swallowed whole, I pulled away and felt teeth scraping against my sweet little cheeks. I ducked out from under the canoe and swam home.

Try explaining teeth marks on either side of your face to your grandma. It became evident that I no longer believed her pregnancy theory.

Looking back on having my face masticated, I wondered if he never practiced on the back of his hand like we girls did in middle school or if some dumb girl said, "Mmm, I like the way you kiss." That would do it. Someone accidentally reinforced his bad behavior by giving him a verbal nod before backing away slowly, turning, and running like hell. He had missed my lips and tried to swallow my face. I don't think it mattered that I was there. It was as though I was just something to chew on for a while, like a bone to a dog, but much less willing.

A kiss like that, like the choke of the tongue-jammer kisser, even at that age, revealed the one-sidedness of anything that came after. He wasn't the guy who would take ballroom dance lessons with me later in life nor would he be up for a couple's pedicure. A kiss like that was a demolition derby to what should have been a sunny-day, top-down on the MG Midget cruise along the A1A. The disappointment was palpable.

"K-I-S-S-I-N-G" is the part *right before* "first comes love." It's the practice prelude to a lifelong commitment of conjoined faces and happily ever after. It's that little plastic doll-sized spoon from which the clerks tease you with gelato samples, toying with your wants and desires of a single scoop or double. I'll take the whole bin and a soup ladle if the sample's good enough.

THAT's where babies come from: gelato.

I don't know. That Jaws kisser gave a whole new meaning to my grandmother's bacon bits of wisdom when she said, "the way to a man's heart is through his stomach." I didn't think it was supposed to be quite so literal.

LOVE BITES
(Cheesecake-Filled Chocolate-Covered Strawberries)

INGREDIENTS:
- 1-lb container strawberries, washed, dried, and hulled
- 1 cup chocolate chips
- 1 tsp coconut oil
- 1 (8 oz) package cream cheese
- ¾ cup powdered sugar
- ¼ cup whipping cream, whipped
- Mint leaves

DIRECTIONS:

Wash and pat the strawberries till dry. Cut the tops off and, using a sharp paring knife, remove the hull. Set aside. Cover a baking sheet with waxed paper.

In a small bowl, combine chocolate chips and coconut oil. Place in a microwave and heat at 20-second intervals until melted. Stir frequently. Dip strawberries in chocolate and place on a cookie sheet. Place cookie sheet in the refrigerator to cool and harden chocolate.

In a small bowl, beat whipping cream until whipped and stiff. In a separate bowl, beat cream cheese and powdered sugar until creamy. Add in whipped cream. Mix until combined. Spoon cream cheese mixture into a plastic bag. Cut a small tip off one corner of the bag and pipe the cream cheese mixture into the prepared strawberries. Garnish with mint leaves.

Chill until ready to serve.

2.

CHEESECAKE LOVES MY THIGHS

Closets are brutal. They're a wasteland of beautiful fabric and busted zippers.

The 37" × 80" hole in the wall in which I hang and fold a so-called wardrobe of thrift-store finds and Nordstrom Rack clearance items, all fit one leg or the other but no longer at the same time. Most shirts only button at the top and, believe me, it's neither because of missing buttons nor is this a boob issue. The saggy size A's have never posed a problem for closing a blouse, jacket, or stretching a T-shirt. It's what used to be called the muffin top but now is more like the layer-cake middle. That's the issue.

My perfectly worn and torn jeans wait for me. They wait for the prodigal size 6, who once upon a time wandered into the kitchen and has never returned. The non-gluten-free bread crumb trail that left the closet behind, spiraled to the snack cabinet filled with plastic-wrapped goodies designed to give the once-upon-a-time sizes the big F-you.

The pull between the expectation of size and the deliciousness of good food has been the tug-of-war on my self-worth almost since graduating out of diapers, making the transition from a onesie to a shawl of shame almost seamless. I don't know how it happened, but I blame the butter.

I blame butter, but we all know that butter isn't really the issue. The issue is that women's bodies have been at the critical, judgmental, and airbrushed scrutiny of merciless glamour ideals ever since the matriarchal sovereignty gave way to the patriarchy for some asinine reason.

Personally, body parts got targeted and my thighs were a bull's-eye.

Newly minted into adulthood, my thighs had already been spurned by men, by me, and even by my mom, who loved to point out when I'd put on a few pounds and where it showed.

Unsolicited advice, ideas, and lessons came my way to address this apparently big issue. From a stretch band for the outer thighs, a thigh master for the inner thighs, to random leg lifts throughout the day, I'd heard it all. Jazzercise, aerobics classes, jumping jacks, jumping rope, and jumping on a few fad diets were all squeezed under the belt of effort.

The worst diet advice came directly from the alcohol inlet I called a friend back in the barmaid days of the early 90s. She said that cigarettes not only helped her to stay rail thin but looked sexy to boot. Beer goggles and a smoked mirror aside, I was gullible, naïve, and desperate enough to give it the ol' college try. The friend failed to mention the taste and neither of us cared about cancer. We were young and dumb and looking to look good or at least better than we felt we looked. I hated smoking. I skivvied and coughed with each puff of the panacea for pear bottoms. It was gross but I kept at it.

Eventually, I traded the cigarettes for a bicycle and things started looking up.

One summer day, after biking across town to my boyfriend's apartment, I draped my legs over his midsection while we talked about what to do that evening. We often spent time in this position, on the beige, carpeted floor, waxing poetically about who we thought we were supposed to be and what we thought we were supposed to do. More accurately, I faux philosophized in a run-on babble while he did … what? I don't know. Maybe he thought about things, too. Maybe he listened. Most likely not, though. On this day, without warning and with great excitement, the conversation turned left without signaling.

He exclaimed, "Good Lord! Your thighs are HUGE!"

And before I knew it, I was toppled ass to the ceiling and flying like a small kitten thrown from a blanket to a new space on the floor. He jumped up, yelled something about crushing a tin can, and ran to the kitchen for an empty can of beer to test his theory. Returning with can in hand, the realization of what he'd just said hit him. He tried to take back his words as quickly as he could, but the wrong ones just kept replacing the right ones as they exited his mouth. After repetitions of "that came out wrong" and "that's not what I meant," he went on to say that he meant I would have a great body if only I worked out. If only. Somewhere between the immediate pain of that insult upon insult and the desire to hide beneath my shame, my mind rattled off a list of "if only's" for him that sounded like an automatic assault rifle inside my head but looked exactly like a slow-forming well of saltwater pooling in my eyes. I can't say what happened next because I'm pretty sure that after my heart broke, my head exploded.

I biked home, angry and filled with self-doubt, swearing that this time I was done. But I wasn't. I stuck with him the way I stuck with cigarettes. I stayed despite the thigh-slapping jabs and pokes in the belly. Offers to work out together continued and we spent time negotiating the finer points of iceberg lettuce with or without ranch dressing.

My thighs may have been strong like an Olympic deadlifting champion, but my resolve, like my self-worth, was still made of Jell-O.

In a vortex of self-deprecation, I convinced myself that if my thighs were thinner our bond would be thicker; that his love for me would grow the more I shrank. There was little anyone could do to convince me that my thighs weren't really the issue.

But cheesecake loves my thighs. Cheesecake loves my butt, my hips, and my belly, too. Cheesecake loves a walk that makes a "ka-boom, ka-boom" with a bit of "ba-donk-a-donk" from the backside. It loves curves that make a body bodacious.

Cheesecake loves bodacious. It loves fat. It's full of fat.

I will unapologetically repeat that: Fat.

Fat carries and distributes the flavor while, at the same time, giving cheesecake its silky texture. The fat in cheesecake is like scent for a rose, like sweetness in honey, and like curves on a woman. It's a part of what makes cheesecake *cheesecake* and part of what makes cheesecake love my thighs. Like attracts like.

Cheesecake doesn't think that I should work out; it will only ask me to lift a fork and crush graham crackers for a crust. Cheesecake isn't going to make me feel less of who I am because I'm more of what it thinks I should be.

Whether I am rail thin or shopping double X's, cheesecake will always love my thighs.

Another time, this same boyfriend wondered how much weight my legs could press. Instead of lifting me up and making me feel beautiful, he asked me to lay on the ground with my feet in a tabletop position. He wondered if I could leg lift *him* which, similar to "are you PMS-ing?" "Want to split the bill?" and "How long have you been on Weight Watchers?" is a question no girlfriend ever wants to hear. He placed himself on top of my feet, wide-eyed and full of wonder just like an eight-year-old boy in the freak-show tent of a traveling carnival. I was the main attraction. He insisted I lift, and like a good carny, I did. It wasn't just a lift. I let my freak fly and I launched him. I mean I REALLY launched him. He was not prepared for his sudden flight across the room.

Don't mess with the can crusher.

THE CAN CRUSHER
(Brown Butter Cheesecake)

INGREDIENTS:

Crust
- 2 cups graham crackers
- 1 cup almonds
- ⅓ cup sugar
- ½ cup butter, melted

Cheesecake
- 3 (8 oz) packages cream cheese, room temperature
- ½ cup butter (1 stick), melted and browned
- 1 T vanilla extract
- 1 (8 oz) container sour cream
- 1 cup sugar
- ¼ cup brown sugar
- ¼ cup heavy cream
- 4 eggs

DIRECTIONS:

Preheat oven to 350° F. Grease the bottom and sides of a 9" springform pan. For crust, place almonds and graham crackers into a food processor and pulse until they are crumbs. Add sugar. Pulse until blended. Transfer to a bowl. Add butter. Combine until the mixture holds together. Press the mixture into the bottom and sides of the springform pan. Bake at 350° for 10 minutes. Set aside to cool.

Wrap the cheesecake pan in a double layer of aluminum foil, and place into a large, deep baking pan to prepare for the water bath.

In a saucepan, melt the butter. With heat set to high, stir the butter and bring it to a boil. When it begins to turn brown, remove it from the heat and continue to stir until it is a caramel-brown color. Set aside to cool.

In a bowl, mix cream cheese and sugar until smooth. Add sour cream, brown sugar, and butter, one at a time, and mix until blended. Scrape sides of the bowl often to ensure even mixing. Add vanilla extract. Mix. Add eggs, one at a time, and mix on slow until blended. Pour over prepared crust and place in the baking pan. Add hot water to the baking pan so it reaches about 1" up the side of the springform pan. Carefully place pan with cheesecake in the preheated oven and bake for 60–75 minutes or until sides are set and center jiggles. Turn off the oven and allow cheesecake to slowly cool in the warm oven for 30 minutes.

Remove from oven and cool to room temperature (about 2 hours). Run a knife along the inside edge of the pan to release the cheesecake and prevent cracking. Refrigerate at least 6 hours or until ready to serve.

Top with fresh fruit of your choice.

3.

ALL CHEESECAKE IS RICH ... VERY RICH

Everybody wants to be rich. The only people who don't want a ridiculous amount of money are the people who already have it.

Even when I was a child, the fantasy of wealth and the easy life it would provide was a vision shared by me and every other kid I knew. We didn't play 'pauper' or 'middle-class-family scenario' or 'hide in the double-wide.' We played 'princess' and we wore fake tiaras and plastic pearls and drank tea with a pinky finger up in the air, just as we were shown to do by Disney. Or Mattel. Barbie had a Malibu dream house and I wanted one, too. Her house had an elevator. She drove a pink convertible. Doll companies never made a Barbie-sized, faded silver-and-tan conversion van with floor-to-ceiling maroon carpet and swivel chairs for Barbie's pot-smoking friends and their toothless cronies. Barbie's sports car had her logo on it and it seated two: Barbie and her sculpted man-toy with perfect teeth.

In elementary school, my friends and I gathered at recess to play MASH-up. This game told us who we would marry, what type of house we would live in, how many kids we'd have, and what car to drive. Between this game, paper fortune tellers, and the Magic 8 Ball, we could predict with ten-year-old accuracy, a certain future of our love lives and adulthoods. Fate, it seemed, was in the palm of our hands. The letters M.A.S.H. stood for Mansion, Apartment, Shack, House.

The game was simple: List in quantities of four, from the most awful to the most sublime, details about your future. Depending on how the game unfolded, your future might foretell marrying a rich celebrity or your friend's stupid kid brother. You might be driving a red Porsche or a rusty jalopy. We played this game endlessly with new predictions for our future with every number picked between one and ten and with each line through and circle around. I remember none of the actual results but do remember that we all wanted to be rich. None of us fourth-grade girls were hoping for a mobile home on cinder blocks, thirteen ratty kids and a deadbeat husband named Billy-Bob. We all wanted to live in a mansion.

Television confirmed our desires with shows like *Lifestyles of the Rich and Famous* and *Dynasty*. Each week, the host of the *Lifestyles* show, Robin Leach, showed the houses and cars of the world's richest people. These homes had colonnades, marble floors, a lot of leaded windows, and always a fountain behind a gated drive. He never show-cased a house like mine: a 1970s ranch decked out in the most average 1970s country-blue gingham curtains, brown plaid furniture, and oval rag rugs that the local 'antique' stores had to offer. We weren't rich. My single mom drove a wobbly, mustard-colored station wagon with three scrawny kids scrapping it out in the wayback. From what I could tell, rich people didn't wear hand-me-downs or play Hula-Hoop in the sprinkler. Rich people didn't have oscillating lawn sprinklers at the end of the green garden hose. They had irrigation systems on timers. Rich people didn't have a short, scruffy mutt with a cute name like "Fluffy." They had Afghan hounds named for regions of wine. Rich people were married and vacationed in Morocco. I wanted that, too.

We all wanted that. Even in fourth grade we knew we wanted that.

But somewhere along the line, Robin Leach retired, and *Dynasty* went off the air. My dreams of being whisked away in my private jet with my real-life version of the six-million-dollar man to a quaint café in Paris took a backseat to a handful of regular, ol' American French fries from a drive-through.

Café au lait and *s'il vous plait* went to "pardon my French" in the hangnail days of minimum-wage labor. For a while I forgot about being rich and focused on making enough cash to put gas in my car so I could get to that minimum-wage job so I could put gas in my car. It felt like an endless loop, but I had hopes it was really a lasso for a better life in disguise.

The concept of becoming rich felt as realistic as making it to China by digging a hole in the backyard.

Drive a jalopy equals meet a mechanic. Work in the mall equals dinner in the food court. Dreaming bigger became the result of setting standards lower. This was the low-income math that I like to refer to as "learning the value of a dollar." I would have liked to learn this value in a fancier way, but commuter college only afforded so much stretch to the imagination.

In those days, I felt like I was dating well if the guy took me out for dinner and it wasn't at the family-style restaurant next to the Baker's Pie across from the gas station. My friends and I, all with similar socioeconomic status, were feeling pretty fancy if our dates wore a shirt with buttons.

We fell in love with potential. Like ancient astronomers, we thought we could see stuff that wasn't there by connecting dots in the sky a universe away. I saw a better life for us all. Robin Leach, in my certainty, was waiting to come out of retirement so he could tell our tales of ridiculous wealth and show our grotesquely fancy houses to the rest of the world for inspiration.

A few years after I should have known better, I developed a crush on a coworker. He was just this side of my mom saying, "Oh, honey—don't touch that. We'll call animal control." But he was also the only male in the workplace of testosterone-thirsty, fix-it-all, momma-drama wannabes. To be fair, he was handsome. He just didn't own a tennis racquet or a lemon-yellow cardigan to tie around his shoulders.

He feasted on plastic-wrapped Honey Buns and cigarettes and had a faint cologne of yesterday's bender. I fantasized about what fresh vegetables, a hot shower, and some running shoes might do to clean up that man-mess.

Most days for lunch, he'd get fast food while I was trying to fill up on rabbit snacks. The smell of his French fries held the same appeal as heated leather seats in the car I dreamt of owning. I tried not to drool. His dollar-menu burger looked like filet mignon. One day, he leaned over and asked if I wanted his fries as he handed over the entire lot. No answer needed. No more questions asked. I smiled like that kid I used to be and ate them all without ever looking away from the grease-stained bag they came in.

Shame, along with the fries, immediately settled in the pit of my stomach. I never imagined myself getting so aroused by a bag of fries. Things were more desperate than I was willing to admit. *Merde.*

My coworker continued giving me his fries. He gave them to me every time we had lunch together. Every. Single. Time. I never asked for them and I took this gesture as a clear sign of interest on his part. I assumed that my acceptance of his fries meant that the show of interest was reciprocal. He was speaking my love language: food.

With French fries came a side order of hope in a basket next to "I can fix this." I flirted with the idea for tacos but got more fries. I crossed my fingers for a real dinner instead of leftover lunch and got more fries. It took a while, but my quiet optimism wore him down or maybe it was the bloat that had settled into my heavily salted cheeks. He didn't actually ask me on a date but did offer to 'hang out' sometime. We did. I called it dating. He called it not dating. Po-TAY-to. Po-TAH-to. On our first non-date, he offered to drive me to the repair shop where my car was clinging on for dear life and where his car needed to retire. I had hoped to be picked up for the non-date without him first crawling through the passenger-side door because the driver's-side door of his truck didn't open. I yearned to be in some other vehicle of his where it didn't take two people and a stick to start it on a count of three. I prayed that the ride would include dinner. It didn't.

I saw his shiny potential chip away like cheap nail polish. With each bag of French fries and every non-date, I'd hoped he'd get some grist in his grind and get us going to the *Dynasty* way of dating and leave the fries behind. He didn't.

I kept hope alive as long as I could, but my health was at risk.

Coming away from a non-date, or any date, smelling like fried food and engine grease was not what I had circled on the MASH-up game. If I was going to be offered something French, it had best come from a waiter in Paris and not from guy in the drive-through window at McDonalds.

French fries are fine, but they aren't cheesecake. Cheesecake is rich; very rich. It's not five-dollar-an-hour poor. Cheesecake is *Lifestyles of the Rich and Famous* rich. Cheesecake is the rich I had been preparing for.

LIFESTYLES OF THE RICH AND FAMOUS
(Saffron and Orange-Blossom Cheesecake)

INGREDIENTS:

Crust
- 2 cups gingersnap cookies
- 1 cup pistachios, chopped
- 2 T all-purpose flour
- ½ cup butter, melted

Cheesecake
- 4 (8 oz) packages cream cheese, room temperature
- ½ cup sugar
- ½ cup raw honey or orange-blossom honey
- ½ tsp vanilla extract
- 2 T orange-blossom water
- 2 T orange zest
- Pinch of ground saffron threads
- Pinch of turmeric
- 1 T vodka
- 4 large eggs plus 2 yolks, room temperature
- ¼ cup sour cream
- ¼ cup heavy cream
- 2 T cornstarch

Topping
- ⅓ cup orange marmalade
- 1 T orange-blossom water
- ½ cup sour cream
- Candied orange peels, chopped into small pieces
- Fine sugar for dusting

DIRECTIONS:

Preheat oven to 350° F. Grease the bottom and sides of a 9" springform pan. For crust, place nuts into a food processor and pulse until they are crumbs. Add cookies and pulse again. Add flour to the mix. Pulse until blended. Transfer to a bowl and add butter. Combine until the mixture holds together. Press the mixture into the bottom and sides of the springform pan. Bake at 350° for 10 minutes. Set aside to cool.

Wrap the pan in a double layer of aluminum foil, and place in a large, deep baking pan to prepare for the water bath.

In a small bowl, combine saffron, turmeric, and vodka. Let soak until ready to use.

In a bowl, mix cream cheese and honey together until smooth. Add orange-blossom water, vanilla, and sugar, and beat on low until smooth. Add sour cream, cornstarch, and zest. Blend. Add in vodka, saffron, and turmeric mixture. Blend. Add eggs, one at a time, and mix until blended.

Pour over prepared crust. Add hot water to the baking pan so it reaches about 1" up the side of the springform pan. Carefully place the pan with the cheesecake in the preheated oven and bake for 60–75 minutes or until sides are set and center jiggles.

In a saucepan, heat marmalade and orange-blossom water, whisking until melted and smooth. Add sour cream. Whisk together. Pour over cheesecake. Turn off oven and let the cheesecake rest for 30 minutes in the oven.

Remove from oven and cool to room temperature (about 2 hours). Run a knife along the inside edge of the pan to release the cheesecake and prevent cracking. Refrigerate for 6 hours or until ready to serve.

Sprinkle the bits of candied orange peel around the edge of the cheesecake and dust with sugar.

Serve and enjoy.

4.

CHEESECAKE ISN'T CHEAP

Cheapskates are the worst. Frugal I get because it's like being cash poor but creativity rich, but cheap is more irritating than sand in your swimsuit. Taking time to make a gift because you don't have money to buy something is frugal. Not buying or giving a gift because you don't want to spend the money is cheap.

Cheap and cheesecake simply don't go together. You might not have the money for graham crackers and instead you use the cookie stash in the pantry, but that doesn't make the cheesecake cheap. It makes you an outside-the-box thinker, unafraid to take a few risks.

Cheesecake is about investing your time and energy. They take an hour to bake and two more to cool which means that this type of baking is not for the impatient. It's not kindergarten-teacher patient, but it's wonder-where-your-dinner-delivery-is patient. This effort of time is what makes cheesecake so rich and so wonderful.

I had high hopes for this kind of wonderful when I met a man at a dinner party sometime between French fries and marriage; a man with dark hair, dark eyes, and a look that was a midwestern, everyday, real-people version of young Sean Connery handsome. When he walked into the room, there was a collective inhale. All eyes were on the dreamboat. He was armed with a smile and two bottles of wine—one red and one white, prepared for anything that the evening might offer.

"He volunteers," they said.

"He's a good guy," they said.

"He's got some quirks," they said.

They were right on all accounts.

A quirk, for a guy who looked like 007, seemed like it should fall under the category of a navel-fuzz collection. That's quirky. He was badass-handsome enough to make any quirk inconsequential. In my mind, I felt that he was so out of my league with those looks that if he looked my way, I would overlook just about anything.

He asked me for a date before dessert was served, and I, in full earnest, asked if he was serious. Filled with disbelief, I silently wondered if *that* was his quirk: escort alms for the average and often overlooked. Maybe it's a tax-deduction. He was serious. Then I wondered if maybe he was hired … you know … like an escort … to be my date.

Mentally, I began to titivate my old wardrobe and assess all the ways I wasn't good enough. I haven't read enough of the right books. My retirement fund depended on winning the lottery and my financial worth diminished by two dollars every week as I hung on to hope for a win. I wished I would have kept my New Year's resolution. I felt grossly inadequate and immediately unkempt. I'd need a seamstress and a hairdresser. Stat.

The mall called. They had just the thing that I needed to buy that I would later regret. A sale-rack shopping spree and a girlfriend fashion consultation were crammed into the frenetic space between the "Sure. That's sounds great," and "Hello, again." I was just hoping to look good enough to meet my expectations of what I thought his expectations might be. I wished I hadn't let the yoga studio membership lapse … years ago.

Walking into the restaurant of his choosing, a pub, 007 sent me to the bar so he could have a conversation with the hostess. My thoughts immediately spun around what special thing he was planning to do to impress me. Would there be singing? Would there be a candle in my dessert? I searched the floor for rose petals.

The hostess was a smooth character. She made no subtle gestures to signal his next move. Nothing special happened during dinner. The burger he encouraged me to order instead of the salmon entrée I had wanted was not as special as he made it sound. It was fine. I suspected the salmon must have been poisoned because the burger was just a burger. Nothing special happened after dinner when we didn't order dessert. He talked me out of dessert for reasons that will soon become clear. No one sang. No candle burned. No ninja-bad-guy dropped down on wires from the ceiling. It's okay. I was a trooper. I was still aflutter over the mystery meeting with the hostess.

When the bill came, the mystery was solved. He pulled out his *GROUPON*. That's what he wanted to talk to the hostess about: the Groupon! That's why he didn't want us to get dessert. It wasn't included on the Groupon. That's why we came to the pub for burgers. One burger was free.

I sucked in half of my bottom lip and bit down, feeling a bit like a bargain-basement reject.

Groupon is a great thing, don't get me wrong … but maybe not on a *first* date! It put a cap on our wants and desires, restricting them to the items listed in the small print. The first date is the time of wooing, and wooing seems like it should feel unobstructed, not discounted. It left me feeling like I was not worth any sort of investment. I wasn't worth the full price of a burger. My perceived worth was less than ten dollars. Even I knew I was worth more than that. Hell, my mani-pedi cost four times that and he never even looked at my nails.

Discounted dating happens after your bank accounts merge, and you are saving for something specific like a trip to Fiji or a house or a family car that can pull a boat. Discounted dating happens when I stop putting so much effort into how I look, and you get to see the hair in braids, the face with no makeup and a body draped in overalls.

As someone who drives a fuel-efficient can on wheels, I understand the economy of things wanted versus afforded, but it felt like the discounted date was more a matter of disposition.

I could have overlooked frugality, but it turned out that *Mr. Diamonds are Forever* was more like *Mr. Cubic Zirconia are temporary and crack easily.*

After he paid for our dinner with a Groupon, he left a tip based on the *discounted amount*, indicating that the waitstaff wasn't worth much, either.

On the way home, he asked if I wanted to go somewhere for a glass of wine and promptly pulled out two bottles of wine from the back seat: one red and one white. I asked if he, by chance, loved that wine since those were the same vintage that he'd brought to the party.

He said no. They WERE THE SAME BOTTLES. He said, "Since no one drank them at the party, I brought them home. I bought them. They're mine."

Not even the hosts of the party were worthy of his gratitude. This was someone who would have given me one French fry and only if I asked. He probably would have asked me to pay him back.

My girlfriends at the Monday night cheesecake events would have had a field day with the B-class stunt double. Bottom line is that he didn't feel I was worth it, nor was anyone else.

Every slice of cheesecake tells you that you are worth it.

Every indulgent forkful tells you that you, beautiful you, are worth every penny and every minute that it took to make that cheesecake.

THE 007

(Chocolate and Vanilla Cheesecake with Chocolate Ganache)

INGREDIENTS:

Crust

- 2 cups chocolate wafer cookies
- ½ cup walnuts
- ⅓ cup sugar
- ½ cup butter, melted

Cheesecake

- 3 packages (8 oz each) of cream cheese, room temperature
- ½ cup honey
- ¼ cup sugar
- 1 T cornstarch
- 2 tsp vanilla extract
- 3 large eggs plus 2 yolks, room temperature
- 3-oz dark chocolate bar, melted

Topping

- ⅓ cup orange marmalade
- 2 T water

Ganache

- 2 cups chocolate, chopped fine
- 1 cup heavy cream

DIRECTIONS:

Preheat oven to 350° F. Grease the bottom and sides of an 8" springform pan. In a food processor, pulse the walnuts and the cookies until they are crumbs. Add sugar and pulse until blended. Transfer to a bowl and add butter. Combine until the mixture holds together. Press the mixture into the bottom and sides of the springform pan. Bake at 350° for 8 minutes. Set aside to cool.

Wrap the pan in a double layer of aluminum foil, and place in a large baking pan to prepare for the water bath.

In a large bowl, beat cream cheese with honey until smooth. Add sugar and vanilla. Beat until smooth. Add eggs and egg yolks, one at a time, mixing until fully combined. Scrape sides of bowl often. Add cornstarch and mix. Divide cheesecake batter in half. Mix chocolate into one-half of the batter mixture and blend until smooth.

Pour chocolate batter on top of the crust. Spoon vanilla on top of the chocolate layer and smooth top with back of spoon. Add hot water to the baking pan so it reaches about 1" up the side of the springform pan. Carefully place pan with cheesecake in the preheated oven and bake for 60–75 minutes or until sides are set and the center jiggles. Turn off oven and allow cheesecake to slowly cool in the warm oven for 30 minutes. Remove from oven.

On low heat, melt orange marmalade and water. Pour over cheesecake. Let cool to room temperature. Run a knife along the inside edge of the pan to release the cheesecake and prevent cracking. Refrigerate for 6 hours or until ready to serve.

Remove cheesecake from springform pan.

To make ganache, chop chocolate into fine pieces and place in a small bowl.

In a small saucepan, heat cream until steaming. Pour hot cream over chocolate and let sit for 5 minutes. Stir. Continue stirring until all the chocolate is melted and the mixture is smooth. (If more heat is needed, place bowl into a larger bowl that has hot water in the bottom.) Pour over cheesecake. Refrigerate until ready to serve.

5.

BREAKING UP WITH CHEESECAKE IS ...

JUST KIDDING.

NO ONE EVER BREAKS UP
WITH CHEESECAKE

"Oh, no he didn't," "Oh, yes, he did," "Girl, be done." The sequence is familiar because it's the one we have all had with our girlfriends. You know the look on your girlfriend's face during the exchange. Sometimes, the look is sadness. It feels like big-sister-kicking-someone's-ass protection with a side of softness like a mom hug. The expression, however, is one of disappointment because one more heart has been broken.

When I was younger, breakups were unpredictable in my somewhat melodramatic reactions. I didn't know how to control my natural inclination toward dramatic flair. The devastation felt insurmountable and took a long time from which to recover. Restoration was mainly about figuring out how to stuff the feelings into my underwire and pretend that nothing was askew. Regardless of who broke up with whom, there was some ugly involved on my end. Sometimes, this was fixed with a face wash and a reapplication of mascara, but usually not. It was deeper than that.

Breakups, I've learned, come in a variety of flavors. There's the *Empowerment Breakup,* where he drops subtle clues that the relationship is over until you finally take the hint and end it. He acts surprised but he's not. There's the *Disappearing Act.* It's self-explanatory. There's the *Easy-Let-Down.* It starts with "Listen…" There's the *Blamer* who insists he has done great things for you, GREAT things, but that none of them were good enough because your expectations were too high. This is the guy who blames you, shames you, often berates you, and then pleads with you to take him back. After all, who wouldn't want a guy back who's just tested the extent of his explicit vocabulary on your self-worth? Then there's the *Surprise Ending.* He didn't see it coming. You didn't see it coming. Maybe neither of you saw it coming. Either way, it happened and there you have it. This is the breakup rooted in fear, but which impersonates banalities such as the toilet seat being left up or the smell of his gym bag from anywhere in the house. It jolts you like gas from yesterday's ethnic food when you reach down to tie your shoe.

In the case of the thigh-master boyfriend, rather than ditching the dude, I was going to diet. Losing weight felt like a better option than losing love. I swore that I was done with delicious food for good. No more decadent, melt-in-your-mouth goodness of melted cheese in the macaroni. No more Cool-Whip filler between meals. No more calling an ice-cream sandwich lunch. I put the fork down. Done. Over. I was going back to the weight it said on my driver's license.

One salad later the regret sank in like a warm Jell-O on poke cake.

After almost one hundred Sundays together, the two of us went out for our typical Sunday brunch: there was a buffet; there were mimosas. He began the conversation by talking about the taboo topic of my impending graduation. I wasn't having it. I wasn't going to entertain the idea of growing up by talking about finishing college. I postponed graduation indefinitely. The boyfriend wanted to talk about *that.* He wanted to plan for a *future.* I wasn't ready for a future. I wasn't done with college. I hadn't taken basket weaving yet. African Dance was only offered in the fall. I had to go for one more year. The student loans were waiting for my deferment plan.

There was no way he could have ever seen the panic overwhelm me. Inside my head were next year's offering of classes, each one flashing like a vacancy sign in the eternal vacation of delayed academic achievement. The words were building up pressure like a shaken can of soda. The top popped.

I looked at my perfect boyfriend and said, "I don't think we should see each other anymore."

He froze like a deer in the headlights the moment before the Mack Truck runs him over. I kept on truckin' and told him something along the lines of "this just doesn't feel right."

He sat motionless for a long time. Not one for arguments, with a subtle nod and a quiet, "Okay," he left.

As the restaurant door closed behind him, the dam broke. Head in hands and salty tears running down to my elbows, I wailed. I never saw that coming. I continued to wail long after the waiter asked me to leave.

The boyfriend never looked back. He was gone. I didn't see that coming, either. He was supposed to come back. He was supposed to understand that the words came out wrong and what I meant to say was ... but he was gone.

It was my first major breakup though not the first time I had felt abandoned by someone I loved. The feeling was becoming too familiar, and I was miserable. I was young. I didn't know about the phoenix yet. I didn't know that love would come again so I stayed in my misery wondering why he didn't come back.

The saying is that misery loves company. I discovered that misery doesn't love company. It loves cheesecake.

One dreary Monday in Wisconsin, I had learned the cure for the broken heart.

I lived in an old Victorian house with four other coeds. Aside from Ruth, who was studying to become a nun, the rest of us were routinely in and out of relationships. Two of those relationships ended up in marriage (three if you include Ruth's vows to God).

For months after the breakup, while my roommates were all out with their dates—except for Ruth, who was in her room courting God—I was just a lump of blankets and used tissues, often on the floor of my bedroom. Monday nights, the blanket pile that was me relocated to the living room to watch *Northern Exposure*. Each week, I waited for Joel and Maggie to break their tension with a kiss. Hope also emerged that *THIS* week John Corbett would cure my sadness by climbing through the television, wrapping his arms around me, and taking my heartache away with …

Watching *Northern Exposure* meant ordering pizza. One fateful night, dessert came with the pie. The guy on the phone said they had cheesecake. It was included.

Recalling the cheesecake from my childhood, I was in no mood for sugar and canned cherries but refusing took too much effort.

The pizza arrived along with another box bearing cheesecake. To my surprise, the cheesecake was not square! In all my twentysomething years, I had only known cheesecake made in a 13" × 9" pan and cut in squares. There were no cherries on top. My mind was blown. All my life, cheesecake and cherry cheesecake were as synonymous as prime rib on Saturday night and ham sandwiches on Sunday after service at church luncheons.

I stared at the cheesecake for quite some time, contemplating all that was wrong with this picture. This wasn't cheesecake. This wasn't what I didn't agree or didn't not agree to have delivered free with my pizza. But it had redemption value: it was free, and it had chocolate on it.

A fork made its way to the chocolate, skimming it off the top like something sacred. Then I tiptoed the fork prongs into the cheesecake like it was Brussel sprouts and I was five. Into my mouth it went, eyes closed, and face already scrunched up, prepared to hate it.

Here's what I learned: This was *BAKED* cheesecake, and it was divine! It didn't come from a box labelled "Jell-O." This was creamy and rich and unlike anything I had ever tasted in my entire life. I fell in love—truly in love—for the first time … with cheesecake.

I became obsessed. Questions came up: What made this so heavenly? Why was it shaped in a wedge? Could I make this? What ex-boyfriend?

I had a new mission. Answers to my cheesecake questions were out there. I just had to find them. This was pre-Internet 1991, which meant I picked up the only phone that existed and physically dialed numbers. I called everyone in my address book and asked for cheesecake recipes. Recipes came in the mail by the dozens, each with a note claiming *this* recipe to be the best.

I've yet to master the original bliss of that first cheesecake. It's like trying to re-create a first kiss. Even without the anticipation or the romantic tension, each recipe mended my heart a little more. The more I baked, the better I felt.

The learning curve was steep. I learned that you could say stuff you don't mean to a cheesecake, and it doesn't walk away. And the only tears you will cry in a restaurant are ones of joy when the waitstaff brings you another piece of cheesecake.

THE BREAKUP

(Vanilla Bean Cheesecake with Cracked Chocolate Topping)

INGREDIENTS:

Crust

- 1 cup walnut pieces, roasted
- 2 cups graham crackers
- 2 tsp cocoa powder
- ½ cup sugar
- 6 T unsalted butter, melted

Cheesecake

- 3 (8 oz) packages cream cheese, room temperature
- 1¼ cup sugar
- ½ cup sour cream
- 1 T vanilla extract
- ½ tsp almond extract
- ½ tsp vodka
- 1 vanilla bean, split lengthwise, seeds scraped
- 3 large eggs plus one egg yolk, room temperature

Topping

- 1 cup semisweet chocolate chips
- 2 T coconut oil

DIRECTIONS:

Preheat oven to 350° F. Butter sides and bottom of a 9" springform pan. In a food processor, pulse the walnuts until ground. Add the chocolate wafers and cocoa powder. Pulse until they are crumbs. Add sugar and mix. Transfer to a bowl. Add the butter and combine until the mixture holds together. Press the mixture into the bottom and sides of the springform pan. Bake for 8 minutes. Set aside to cool.

Wrap the pan in a double layer of aluminum foil, and place pan in a large baking pan and fill the baking pan with 1" hot water to prepare for the water bath.

In a small bowl, place almond extract, vanilla extract, and vodka. Soak the vanilla bean. When it is softened, split the bean, scrape the seeds out and return the seeds to the liquid mixture. Set aside.

In a large bowl, beat the cream cheese with sugar until smooth. Add the sour cream. Beat in the eggs, one at a time, scraping down the sides in between additions. Add the vanilla-bean liquids and blend. Pour the cheesecake batter into the prepared pan. Bake at 350° for 65–75 minutes. The edges will be golden and the center slightly jiggly. Turn off oven and allow cheesecake to slowly cool in warm oven for 30 minutes.

Remove from oven and cool to room temperature (about 2 hours). Run a knife along the inside edge of the pan to release the cheesecake and prevent cracking. Once cheesecake is cool, prepare chocolate topping.

In a microwave-safe bowl, combine the chocolate chips and coconut oil. Microwave for 20 seconds and stir. Continue to microwave and stir at 20-second intervals until chocolate chips are melted and smooth. Pour over cheesecake, creating a very thin layer of chocolate on top. Refrigerate until ready to serve.

Prior to serving, use the back of a spoon to tap the chocolate layer, cracking it into pieces.

(Chocolate can also be cut carefully with a knife that has been heated by running it under hot water.)

6.

CHEESECAKE IS MEANT TO BE SHARED

The first few cheesecakes I made were all mine. They were a part of my grieving process and were meant to make me feel better. I wanted to be left alone with a fork and the contents of the springform pan.

With four other people in the same house at the time of this lament, keeping food to myself was futile.

We all know how that goes. The kitchen is a karmic portal, the manifestation of Murphy's law. It is where the secret ingredients are hidden behind the salt and the sweet of life. It is the space where solitude invites everyone in; one small hush of a spatula against the side of a bowl and the flash mob appears and breaks into chorus. One molecule of flavonoid drifts into the air and a flood of followers arrives, looking at the stove as if it were a messiah. The kitchen is the place where the more one tries to keep something to oneself, the more public it becomes. No note in the world is going to stop the hungry from a leftover slice of pizza ... much less a cheesecake.

The cheesecakes, marked with bright yellow sticky-note warnings and implied threats should they be consumed by anyone other than me, disappeared. They dwindled down to nothing faster than a snowman on a summer day. They evaporated like food does when living with four hungry, boundaryless college students.

Ruth, the future nun, was blamed the most for the missing cheese-cake. She didn't actually do it, but the other roommates accused her of trying to commune with God through cheesecake—much like the rest of us would bribe the house cat to like us by giving it milk. Ruth's relationship with God was far better than any of our relationships with the cat.

Surrendering, I raised a formerly white kitchen towel high in the air and exchanged my bib and fork of solitude for a serving plate and napkins.

Looking back, I laugh at how awful the cheesecakes were and how readily they were consumed. The cheesecakes were lumpy because, be-tween a household of adult wannabes, we didn't own a mixer strong enough to break up the cream cheese. The flavor and texture were in-consistent because I didn't know about having ingredients at room tem-perature. The cheesecakes had cracks on the top from getting too hot too soon or were simply undercooked because "jiggly" can mean so many different things. I followed recipes, but apparently not very closely. A springform pan was more foreign to me than a savings account. Like adulting and like dating, the learning curve for baking was steep.

For however immature my culinary skills, these cheesecakes were still infinitely better than the men we dated, except for, of course, Ruth. Every last crumb of cheesecake was consumed regardless of what it looked like or what step I forgot to follow. No one complained. We just gathered, parceled out the slices as well as the stories, and laughed. We shared time, love, support, and cheesecake.

As weeks passed, the isolation of heartbreak was replaced with the camaraderie of collective experiences. A revolving door of newly minted single friends welcomed in what would come to be known as "the event." It became a thing. Pizza, *Northern Exposure*, and cheese-cake. Blankets on the floor and forks in hand, we regaled tales of dat-ing woes, nightmare boyfriends, diminished self-esteem, and broken hearts, pairing them with biting sarcasm, a little alcohol, and a whole lot of whatever came out of the pan.

In all the stories we shared on Monday nights, we unearthed assumptions and commonalities. We laughed at our "crazy," knowing it was borne from the fertile soil of our discontentment. It wasn't that we were needy, clingy, bitchy, jealous, controlling, demanding, dissatisfied, hard to please, or downright impossible, which is how we were described. Rather, we saw in each other, through the lens of our close bond, that we were questioning the unacceptable, labeling the unjust judgements, and busting through the blame that had been put on each of us to push it back out to where it belonged: clearly on someone else.

Someone wanted to know whatever happened to that artist I had dated. I asked, "Which one?" and threw out some descriptors.

"The tall one with glasses?"

"No."

"The twin with the *hair* and the guitar?"

"No."

"The scrawny blonde with the bounce-house-sized ego?"

Ding! Ding! Ding! A small chorus of "Oh yeah" sounded out as some of us remembered his incredible and grandiose perception of himself. As the details came in about what made him memorable, forgettable, and comparable to cheesecake, one guest wondered about when, exactly, I dated that guy. That particular detail was lost in time, but I did remember a party that we had attended with the mayor.

"You went to the city arts celebration with him and met the mayor?"

"Not the current mayor—the one before this one."

That detail sounded the alarm. My friend went off like a siren. "I was dating him then! I was supposed to go to that party with him! He told me he couldn't take a guest!" And so on until the tears came.

This overlap was news to both of us. Her sadness paralleled my anger and, together, we plotted sweet sagas of revenge. We fantasized that our collusion would be his undoing. We conjured poor reviews for his art exhibits and thought about how we could arrive together, conjoined by papers outlining the dates of our overlap. Consequent Mondays grew the animus like Miracle Gro on water hemlock. We may or may not have driven to his apartment and screamed like banshees. We may or may not have called his house. Whatever we did or didn't do, he simply didn't respond.

We assumed that our wrath ran him out of town, but the reality was that he just wasn't there. He had disappeared faster than the cheesecake and left no crumbs behind. Save one: Ruth. She knew where he was and saw him every day … at the convent. It seemed that Mr. Double-Dip had been hired to teach art to nuns. We could only hope that the cold of the penance pool caused some things to shrivel for this job, which, according to Ruth, also required a promise and dedication to the religious order for which he now worked. It seemed that guy finally found a relationship he could sustain.

Ruth received another slice of cheesecake as an offertory to both her and God.

If only more convents could scoop up the cheaters and have them change their ways, I wouldn't hear the lies of "But she's just a friend" or "I don't know why she keeps texting me photos of herself" or "I know it's Friday night, but I have to work late" or "my mom needs some help this weekend" or insert some other excuse here.

Sharing a boyfriend is not the type of generosity I connect with.

Cheesecake, however, is. When I share cheesecake, no tears are shed. No revenge gets plotted.

Sharing cheesecake is a generous and true act of love.

THE OFFERTORY
(Peach Crumb Cheesecake)

INGREDIENTS:

Crust
- 2¼ cups of graham cracker crumbs (approximately 2½ sleeves of crackers)
- ½ cup salted butter, melted
- 3 T sugar

Cheesecake
- 4 packages (8 oz each) of cream cheese, room temperature
- 1 cup of brown sugar, packed
- 1 T cornstarch
- ½ tsp cinnamon, ½ tsp ginger powder
- ¾ cup sour cream, room temperature
- ¼ cup heavy cream
- 4 large eggs, room temperature

Topping
- Prepared peaches
  - 2 large peaches, pitted and sliced thin
  - Dashes of cinnamon and ginger
  - 2 T brown sugar
- Crumble
  - 1 cup brown sugar
  - ⅔ cup flour
  - ¼ cup crushed pecans
  - 6 T butter, melted

DIRECTIONS:

Preheat oven to 300° F. Grease the bottom and sides of a 9" springform pan. For crust, place graham crackers in a food processor and pulse until they are crumbs. Add sugar to mix. Pulse until blended. Transfer to a bowl and add butter. Combine until the mixture holds together. Press the mixture into the bottom and sides of the springform pan. Bake for 8 minutes. Set aside to cool.

Wrap the pan in a double layer of aluminum foil, and place in a large baking pan for the water bath.

You will need 3 separate bowls for the following: cheesecake, peaches, and crumble

Prepare peaches in a bowl. Mix peaches, cinnamon, ginger, and brown sugar together. Set aside.

Prepare crumble mixture in a bowl. Place sugar, flour, and pecans in the bowl and drizzle with butter. Mix with a fork until lumpy. Set aside.

In a large bowl, beat the cream cheese and the sugar until smooth. Add cornstarch. Add cinnamon and ginger. Mix. Add sour cream and mix in. Scrape the sides of the bowl often to ensure even mixing. Add the eggs, one at a time, and mix in slowly to avoid air bubbles in the batter. Pour one-half of the cheesecake batter into the prepared pan.

Place a layer of prepared peaches on top of cheesecake, using about half of the peaches. Place half of crumble topping on top of peaches.

Pour rest of batter on top of crumble. Layer peaches and crumble again.

Place the prepared cheesecake pan in the large baking pan, and fill the larger pan with 1" water for the water bath. Carefully place in the oven. Bake at 300° for 90 minutes. Turn off oven and let cheesecake cool for half an hour before removing. Remove from oven and cool to room temperature (about 2 hours). Run a knife along the inside edge of the pan to release the cheesecake and prevent cracking.

Refrigerate overnight. Remove from pan and serve.

7.

CHEESECAKE IS WHAT IT SAYS IT IS

A friend asked if I could make her a vegan cheesecake. She's not vegan. She's occasionally vegetarian and this decision usually comes in conjunction with swimsuit season. I get it. Swimsuit season makes kale look pretty tasty.

However, and regardless, the answer is a consistent and adamant no.

Cheesecake is made with cheese and vegans don't eat cheese. Nut "cheese" is a thing but it's not really a cheese. There is no casein in nuts and casein is what makes cheese *cheese*. This is similar to how tofu can be made to resemble beef burgers, but it's still not meat. It will be good, but it won't be the same. A horse with a party hat is not a unicorn and a nut "cheese" cake is not a cheesecake.

Online dating mirrors the idea of vegan cheesecake. You think that what you see on a profile is a good representation of what you are going to get, but a few nibbles in and you know something is off. Online dating profiles are about as accurate in their descriptions as tofurkey is to the taste of real turkey. If you knew your meal was going to be pureed beans instead of carved turkey, you might have taken a hard pass. At least you would have been more prepared for the experience that was about to unfold.

Online dating reminds me of a prank that my grandmother used to play. She made peanut squares, which are layers of vanilla cake, cut into squares, covered in buttercream frosting, and rolled in peanuts. They tasted as sweet as they looked unless you got the one that was actually a frosted block of balsa wood, also rolled in peanuts, and cleverly hidden in plain sight on the platter of real peanut squares.

The platter of online peanut squares is always on the proverbial table and up for grabs. I grabbed one that seemed to align with me politically, spiritually, and socially. This piece of pastry loved animals, bicycling, and cooking. He looked like the real deal. He said he was open-minded and nonjudgmental. The frosting looked sweet. Sold. We agreed to meet over coffee.

Coffee in hand, I ordered a scone. Oh, that scone—all that milk and butter tied in so neatly to flour and sugar and all sorts of other things so many people have decided not to eat.

He gave me a look. You know the one. He asked, "Do you know what's in that thing?" My eyes rolled and my internal voice mumbled some *oh craps*. "Deliciousness." I responded as we settled in at the table.

We weren't two sips into the coffee when he climbed on his righteous soapbox to inform me that what I was eating was precisely what was wrong with people, the environment, and the world today. (Insert more eye-rolling and internal dialogue.)

Another sip of coffee and a bite of scone. Vegan by choice, he found it deplorable that I would dare to eat something made with milk AND butter.

I continued to eat the scone and sip my coffee. The scone was delicious and sweet. His rant had a tone somewhere between tart and mildly angry. I listened but only with one ear as he disrupted my palatial joy with his bitter words.

Protesting over my scone led him on a tangential tirade about Christianity and all folks who attend religious ceremonies. Though he had never, himself, set foot in a church, temple, hut, ashram, or other place of worship, he pontificated that all people who do are just as awful as those who eat animals or animal-derived products or wear leather or, worse, flip flops.

The lecture lasted for as long as I ate my scone. The scone was flaky, sweet, and then gone, except for crumbs. I contemplated licking the plate for punctuation.

I asked him one question that referenced his online profile. "So … you consider yourself open-minded. How so?"

His face puckered in thought, he replied, "I guess you could say that I'm the most closed-minded open-minded person you've met."

It was one of the sweeter things he had said, and I smiled, thanked him for his time as he did mine, and we left the coffee shop.

End of date. I chose the wood block again.

Cheesecake isn't a block of wood disguised as dessert or a dressed-up cream-of-nut. Cheesecake is cheesecake. No big surprise: it's made with cheese just like its name suggests.

THE BIG CHEESE

(Strawberry and Balsamic Reduction Cheesecake)

INGREDIENTS:

Crust
- 1½ cups graham cracker crumbs
- ⅔ cup sugar
- ½ cup butter, melted

Cheesecake
- 4 (8 oz) packages cream cheese, room temperature
- 1¼ cup sugar
- Juice from one lemon
- ½ tsp vanilla extract
- 2 eggs
- 1 T strawberry jam
- 1 T balsamic reduction

Topping
- 1 cup sour cream
- 2 T sugar
- ½ tsp vanilla extract
- 1 tsp balsamic reduction

Balsamic reduction
- ½ cup balsamic vinegar
- ½ cup red wine
- 3 T brown sugar
- Zest of one lemon
- 5 raspberries
- 2 large strawberries, diced
- Plus 5 strawberries sliced thin to marinate in reduction

DIRECTIONS:

To make the balsamic reduction, place all ingredients for reduction in a large saucepan and bring to a simmer. As fruit softens, smash it to release the juices. Simmer until reduced by half. Strain into a bowl. Add sliced strawberries to marinate. Set aside.

Preheat oven to 350° F. Grease the bottom and sides of a 9" springform pan. In a food processor, place broken graham crackers. Process until they are crumbs. Add sugar and pulse until blended. Transfer to a bowl. Add melted butter and combine until the mixture holds together. Press the mixture into the bottom and sides of the springform pan. Bake for 8 minutes. Set aside to cool.

Once cool, wrap the pan in a double layer of aluminum foil, and place in a large baking pan to prepare for the water bath.

In a large bowl, beat the cream cheese until smooth. Add sugar and lemon juice. Beat until smooth. Scrape down sides of mixing bowl often to ensure even mixing. Add vanilla. Beat. Add eggs, one at a time and beat until combined. Pour half of batter into prepared springform pan.

Remove strawberries from marinade and place a layer on top of the batter.

In a small bowl, melt strawberry jam in a microwave for 30 seconds. Add 1 tablespoon of balsamic reduction and mix thoroughly. Spread mixture over strawberries. Spoon remaining cheesecake batter over strawberries. Spread until even. Add approximately 1" of water to large baking pan to create water bath. Carefully place pan in oven and bake for 50–60 minutes until sides are set and center is still jiggly.

In a small bowl, mix the sour cream, sugar, balsamic reduction, and vanilla. Pour over baked cheesecake. Bake for 10 minutes. Turn off oven and allow cheesecake to slowly cool in the warm oven for 30 minutes. Remove from oven and cool to room temperature (about 2 hours). Run a knife along the inside edge of the pan to release the cheesecake and prevent cracking. Refrigerate for 6 hours before serving.

Serve with fresh strawberries and drizzle with balsamic reduction.

8.

NO ONE NEEDS TO TELL YOU WHAT A REAL CHEESECAKE IS

Dressed head to toe in men's camouflage, a rifle on one arm, empty beer cans strewn at my feet, I winced as my oldest brother let out a "Whoop! Whoop!" and snapped a photo of me, outfitted by him, in his hunting finest.

"I promise you that if you use this picture," he said, pride overflowing, "you will have a date by tomorrow."

He advised that I should "know my audience" and stop searching for diamonds in the Lannon Stone quarry.

Advice from my brothers hasn't always been so good. When we were children, my brothers introduced me to a game of lawn darts called Jarts. Jarts, now made with beanbag bottoms, were once upon a time made with steel-tipped daggers and were referred to as "outdoor missiles." They were very different from the indoor ones, clearly. These little hand-tossed missiles were weighted to ensure "they would lodge firmly" into their target, presumably the center space of one of the two small hoops that were pinned to the ground. The pins to our game were no longer in the box, so I, who was too small to throw the hand weapon/toy, was given the job of standing on the lawn hoop so it wouldn't blow away. My brothers exhibited mild concern for my innocent and soft, Twinkie-like feet in the threat of a piercing Jart by advising me to, "just jump out of the way before they hit you."

When I was a little bit older, they insisted I play football with them and the neighborhood boys. Even though I couldn't really catch the ball, I was receiver to their quarterback. My oldest brother knew boys, he said, and touted that none of them would touch me out of fear of our mom being only one of my teardrops away. The touchdowns were too easy for our team, and I was soon kicked out of the game, having been called an unfair tactic.

For much of my childhood, my brothers, though protective and loving, took my femininity as a means of advancing their agendas whether in a game of neighborhood football or asking mom for money for ice cream. They took my size as a physics experiment and launched me from many things to see how high I could go or just to see what would happen. I was spun in a hammock, full circle, until momentum sent me flying many times. A willing participant, I knew the rules in playing with my brothers: no crying, no running to mom, and I had to keep up. They'd help me into the tree we were about to climb, but everything after that was me building strength and resilience. This was mainly a mental exercise. They didn't view me as incapable rather as in need of training.

My brothers were not shy about *not* coddling my softer side. They would not fix anything they thought I could fix myself, including repairs to my teenage appropriate so-called car. I cried and went to mom, but they weren't having it. They taught me how to change my oil, change a tire, clean a carburetor, change a spark plug, and fix a squeaky belt. The middle brother took me to open parking lots in winter so I could practice spinning out. This lesson meant that he randomly yanked the steering wheel or pulled up the emergency brake *to see how I'd handle losing control*. It turns out, I got a lot of practice swearing and screaming.

My brothers' guidance continued to be a bit of a splintered chicken bone in the throat. This latest idea of baiting a better man for me by dressing me in ill-fitting camo I found hard to swallow. As an adult and a self-proclaimed man's man, my oldest brother dressed me, his whisk-wielding, lacy-aproned, "spiders-are-placed-outside-not-squashed" little sister in his deer-hunting finest for a photo shoot intended to land a two-legged buck. He knew men, he said, and this photo would get me one.

Despite his stellar advice, I did not change my profile photo on the dating site. The photo, the site, dating—it all felt so uncomfortable. It felt worse than pantyhose in July or wearing stilettos with socks and bunions. It just wasn't me. I shut it down instead.

But only after I looked just one more time.

I received a wink.

I didn't want a wink. I was shutting the site down.

He was cute.

Dammit.

No. No. Not going to do it.

He sent me his phone number.

Just dammit again.

My willpower to look away, to not engage, had the standing ability of a wet napkin. Suckered in one more time, I distracted myself by wandering into the pantry. *What am I doing?* (Grab the graham crackers …) *Why did I look again?* (the sugar …) *Wasn't I going to shut the site down?* (vanilla …) *Why did I want to date anyway? Wasn't I happy on my own?* (nuts, bowls, mixer …) *Maybe this time things will go more smoothly* (… and the cream cheese.)

Two-legged, online buck was a gentleman. On our first date, when we met at the restaurant, he opened the door for me, saying that a real man opens a door for a lady. I've had doors opened for me before, but I can't say that I've had anyone explain it. I said thank you because one nice gesture deserves another. Conversation was cordial. It was standard-issue awkward but nice enough. When he picked up the tab at the end of the meal he winked and nodded, declaring that a real man picks up the bill, and adding that a lady should never have to pay. I shrugged, and said, "Okay, thank you," even though I had questions. He made another real-man announcement as we left the restaurant, and he walked me to my car, informing me that a lady shouldn't walk by herself. In my head I heard my brothers shout, "She will if she can't keep up!"

The heckling in my mind was getting boisterous as I was trying to decipher if I was just raised wrong—and that I needed so many reminders about what ladies do—or if he thought I wasn't bright or, worse, helpless. As annoying as I found the mansplained manners, I was also a little charmed by them.

I kept my ladylike mouth shut.

The thoughts continued to roll in like an approaching storm. The lady comments and the "real man" statements rumbled in my brain. But then I wondered whether my brother might be right. Perhaps dating someone who defined his character out loud and in clearly outlined boxes wouldn't be so bad. Maybe agreeing to someone who checked the "real man" box would amplify the beauty of living outside it. Maybe this could work.

There was only one way to find out.

By the time of our second date, he began to refer to me as "M'lady" and referred to himself as "Yer man."

"Hello, m'lady. Yer man is here."

Oh. My. Lord. Cute online guy wasn't clued into the fact that terms like "m'lady" went out with jousting. He made me giggle even though I don't think that was his goal.

His vernacular made it appear that John Wayne arrived at my doorstep. There were no chaps, vest, or even a cowboy hat, but the gallantry of his approach had an old western type of flair to it. When I opened the door, he nodded and said, "M'lady." Toe tuck behind the opposite ankle and a quick dip in the knees, I curtsied hello. It felt equal parts playful and ridiculous. The afternoon was spent in this type of frolic as he repeated his duties as a real man, and I pretended to appreciate the chorus. As we walked off our lunch, he had me snapping photos of him next to big trucks high atop oversized, large nub tires while boasting that this is the type of thing a real man drove. According to him, the bigger the truck, the more manly the man.

According to me (and all the women I know), the bigger the truck, the smaller the man parts. He dreamed of these trucks, and I was beginning to fantasize his driving away. It was as close to common ground as we were going to get.

I learned quite a bit about "real" men over the next few dates. I learned that once a man uses a phrase like "real man" he validates all of his thoughts and actions with this label, judging others harshly for not measuring up to his standards of the "real man" box.

The more he spoke, the smaller the box became. He spoke of women's inability to manage money, because, after all, that was a man's job. Men fixed things, he said; women cooked. He added that if women wanted to do man's work like picking up a power tool every now and again, that it would be okay because he found it sexy. Chivalry wasn't dead. It was sexist.

Real-Man was about to meet the can crusher. I wiped the lipstick from my lady mouth, slammed on the emergency brake to this relationship and lost control of the composure that was driving us to each next date.

Real-Man heard a thing or two about my capabilities. I fixed my own chainsaw, hung my own ceiling fans, and cleaned my own gutters. I do cook in my kitchen. It's the one I gutted and then rebuilt all on my own. I have repaired my own car, balanced my checkbook, paid for my own dinners, and opened my own doors ... all without smudging my mascara or breaking a heel.

He listened to my "being hostile" because, as he said, real men understand that "women tend to get too emotional about stuff."

He should have heeded my brother's lawn-Jart advice to "just jump out of the way." My aim had gotten pretty good over the years, but I suspected it was hard for him to hop in those big ol' man boots he wore. I tossed him back in the quarry.

Down the dating site went. No more peeking. No more maybes. No more profile photos to worry about. Closed. Done. Finished. No more listening to my brother, either.

I wandered back to the pantry. *What year did that guy think it was?* (Grab the pretzels ...) *Do I look like I can't take care of myself?* (grab the sugar ...) *Too emotional?* (nuts, vanilla, mixing bowl ...) *Is this what dating has come to?* (... and the cream cheese.) I put it all in a stand mixer and beat the crap out of it.

A REAL MAN'S CHEESECAKE
(Beer and Pretzel Cheesecake)

INGREDIENTS:

Crust
- 1 cup pretzels
- 1 sleeve (about 8 or 9) graham crackers
- ½ cup sugar
- 10 T butter, melted

Cheesecake
- 3 (8 oz) packages cream cheese, room temperature
- 1 cup sour cream
- 1 cup sugar
- ¾ cup stout beer
- 1 T instant coffee
- 2 tsp vanilla extract
- 1 cup chocolate chips, melted
- 4 eggs

Topping
- Stout caramel
  - 1 cup stout beer
  - ½ cup butter
  - 1 cup brown sugar
  - 2 T corn syrup
  - 1 tsp vanilla extract
  - ½ cup heavy cream

Additional topping
- 1 cup whipping cream
- Stout caramel mixture
- Peanuts, crushed

DIRECTIONS:

Preheat oven to 350° F. Grease the bottom and sides of a 9" springform pan. For crust, place pretzels and graham crackers into a food processor and pulse until they are crumbs. Add sugar. Pulse until blended. Transfer to a bowl. Add butter. Combine until the mixture holds together. Press the mixture into the bottom and sides of the springform pan. Bake at 350° for 10 minutes. Set aside to cool. Wrap the pan in a double layer of aluminum foil and place in a larger baking pan to prepare for the water bath.

In a small bowl, mix stout, instant coffee, and vanilla. Set aside. In a separate small bowl, melt the chocolate chips in a microwave, stirring until smooth. Set aside.

In a mixing bowl, beat cream cheese and sugar until smooth. Add sour cream. Add chocolate and mix well, scraping sides and bottom often. Add beer mixture and blend on low. Add eggs, one at a time, and mix on low until blended. Pour over crust and bake for 65–75 minutes or until sides are set and the center jiggles. Turn off the oven and allow the cheesecake to cool slowly in the warm oven for 30 minutes. Remove from oven and cool to room temperature (2 hours).

While cheesecake is cooling, make the stout caramel. In a small saucepan, combine beer and butter and heat until boiling. Reduce heat to medium high and reduce for 8–10 minutes or until it looks opaque and a bit like gravy. Add sugar and corn syrup. Bring back to boiling and cook for about

8–10 minutes more until it coats a spoon. Remove from heat. Stir in vanilla and cream. Bring back to a boil, stirring constantly, for 2–5 minutes
until it thickly coats the back of the spoon. [Caramel sauce can be tested for
stages by having a clear glass of cool tap water and pouring drops of syrup
into the water. If the syrup looks like flakes sinking to the bottom, the syrup
is done. If it enters the soft-ball stage (where it remains a ball at the bottom
of the glass but is squishy when touched), remove from heat and add ¼ cup
more cream. If it enters the hard-ball stage, it has been cooked too long.]
Set aside.

In a small, chilled bowl (over another bowl with ice in it), beat 1 cup
whipping cream until stiff peaks form. Slowly incorporate one-fourth of the
cooled caramel sauce to sweeten the whipped cream. Add more if needed.
Pipe whipped cream around the edge of the cheesecake. Sprinkle with peanuts. Refrigerate until ready to serve.

As each piece is served, drizzle with stout caramel. Enjoy.

9.

THE SIZE OF A CHEESECAKE
IS NOT IMPORTANT

Size matters.

As insensitive as that sounds, it's true. Men are aware and many have size expectations, too. Ask the doctor who wanted to put in "the husband stitch" after I pushed my baby through the birth canal.

Ask my pants the day I walked around accidentally air-conditioning my nether region, because I refused to pay attention to the size I wanted to fit into, versus the size I actually was. That seam split from zipper to beltline, and I couldn't figure out why they had suddenly become so much more comfortable.

Women are fitted for bras. Men are fitted for suits. We are all fitted for bicycles. Even the driver's-side seat moves to accommodate the length of our legs ... because size matters.

My friends and I have talked about this as it relates to dating so much that we no longer need words to express it. Women, in general, have developed an entire set of hand signals, facial tics, and sounds to describe that which no one wants to really say out loud. Beware of the raised pinky finger. We are not exhibiting cult alliance to Dr. Evil.

Think of size as it relates to shoes. If the fit isn't good, you aren't going to buy them or if you do, they aren't going to last long on the favorite shoes list. It doesn't matter what those shoes were made to do. Wrestle, race, or just look damn good. If the shoe doesn't fit, it's not welcome in the closet. No one should buy shoes that are too small. No one … except we all have. We are pulled in by good looks, knowing the fit is bad, wear the shoes once, regret the blisters, and give the shoes away, often with a tinge of regret.

Any woman can relate. Woman have been subject to uncomfortable footwear for eons. We have tortured our feet, misaligned our backs, and hobbled about, blistered and aching. Each time, we tell ourselves that maybe the shoes will stretch out a little bit with time or feel better once we get used to them.

We never get used to a bad fit. We just learn how to fake it better.

Nobody has to fake anything with a cheesecake. 10", 8" or barely a mouthful, it still brings about the same amount of tantalizing, provocative, eyes-rolling-to-heaven, and sincere "Oh-My-God … yes, yes, yes … mmm."

Cheesecake always fits. It fits the situation, the meal, and the mouth. No one has to fake how much they enjoy cheesecake … not even a little bit.

TINY LITTLE NUTSACK

(Baklava Cheesecake Triangles)

INGREDIENTS:

Cheesecake filling

- 1 (8 oz) package cream cheese, room temperature
- ⅓ cup honey
- 1 tsp cornstarch
- 1 T lemon juice
- ½ tsp vanilla extract
- 1 large egg, room temperature

Nut filling

- ½ cup walnuts or pistachios, coarsely chopped
- 2 tsp granulated sugar
- ½ tsp cinnamon
- ¼ cup unsalted butter, melted

Phyllo dough

- 12 sheets at room temperature
- ½ cup butter, melted

Syrup

- ½ cup granulated sugar
- ¼ cup water
- 1 T lemon juice
- 1 cinnamon stick
- 1 T cognac or other brandy

DIRECTIONS:

Preheat oven to 350° F.

Make the filling: In a large bowl, beat the cream cheese until smooth. Add the honey, lemon juice, and vanilla extract. Beat until combined. Add the egg and mix. Add the cornstarch. Blend the ingredients until smooth. Set filling aside.

Make the nut filling: In a food processor, chop the nuts until they are in small bits. Transfer to a bowl. Add sugar, cinnamon, and butter. Mix until combined. Set aside.

To begin assembly, place waxed paper on the countertop to catch butter drips and make cleanup easier. Place one sheet of phyllo dough onto the waxed paper. Using a pastry brush, cover half of the pastry sheet with butter (working lengthwise) and fold the long, unbuttered half onto the buttered half. Coat with butter. Fold the bottom corner of the phyllo pastry to make a triangle. Open. In the crease, place two teaspoons of cheesecake batter. Refold. Fold dough with pastry to make the next triangle and unfold again. Place one teaspoon of nut mixture in the next triangle and refold. Coat with butter and continue to fold phyllo dough into triangles until the end. Coat with butter and place on the cookie sheet. Repeat with remaining phyllo dough, making 12 cheesecake-and-nut-filled triangles.

Bake the triangles for 20 minutes or until golden brown.

In a saucepan, heat sugar, water, lemon juice, and cinnamon stick until sugar dissolves and mixture comes to a boil. Remove from heat. Add cognac or brandy. Stir. Spoon over triangles and serve.

10.

CHEESECAKE DOESN'T HAVE BAGGAGE

It's the empty chair at the table set for four and only three guests that is the issue. No one knows what to do with it. Remove it from the table and it suggests that my friends don't believe I can find a date. Keep it there and it proves they are correct. We single people know the chair. We hate the chair.

The empty chair holds the space for who is or isn't coming much like the lost-and-found area at an airport holds space for unmarked or unclaimed baggage. We all have baggage. We started the collection with a small purse to hold our Bonnie Bell lipsticks along with notes where we learned that our crushes didn't *like*-like us. It has since grown to include a carry-on and a case large enough to hold whatever elephant in the room is traveling with us, too.

Friends want to fill the chair and put the stuff you're dragging with you under the table. They see your baggage and get hopeful about finding someone, somewhere, with a compatible set. They scour the fringes for single men they may have overlooked. They always seem to find one, too.

When the outlier appears, he's typically towing a trailer full of unfinished business, unresolved métier, and a mountain of luggage that have kept his hands and heart occupied for far too long. The load of crap is either blatantly out in the open or it's cleverly veiled behind the eager "I'm a good guy" façade. Either way, it's usually unclaimed.

"I'm not looking for drama" comes up a lot, along with "my crazy ex." I've heard men talk about the gold diggers, robbers, and manipulators as well as the coldhearted, the psychos, and the unhinged. Listening to them gives me the impression that women are all mad as hatters. Maybe we are. Or maybe this is his baggage.

The airlines offer the best advice: Claim it. We know what our baggage looks like. We recognize it as soon as it hits the carousel, and we will squeeze past others to grab what we know is ours.

Emotional baggage, however, gets left behind the rope stanchions near the elevator where it sits with years' worth of other people's unclaimed baggage. Leave it there long enough and the bomb squad comes to blow it up.

A few dates in with a friend of a friend, the guy from the fringe, and someone burst into tears. It wasn't me. The waterworks turned on just before the kiss that never happened. He swore he didn't know why he was crying. I knew it wasn't because of me. I had been on some of my best behavior. Out of a mix of pity, most likely for myself, and curiosity, I continued to date him.

I liked the guy. He was nice; however, more dates brought more tears. Seat belted in his car, standing at the front door, sitting on the couch, he apologized over and over again. So many that they became meaningless. I began to feel like I was the holding place for someone else. That I was somehow hidden and unseen under whatever previous relationship he was denying. I felt like he couldn't see me through the water constantly welling in his eyes. I was but a blur. I stopped waiting for a kiss and just kept a little packet of tissues in my purse.

Admittedly, I had gawker's block. Spending time with him felt like going to NASCAR. No one goes to that race because watching cars go fast and turn left is fun. They don't go for the fumes. People go to NASCAR because they expect to see a car-flipping crash and a guy crawl out from the flames and give a little wave. It's the crash that draws the crowd. These dates were my personal NASCAR. And, like NASCAR, the appeal wore off rather quickly. He became as predictable as a Pringle.

One evening, in what I assume was frustration, he threw himself on the ground, back arched, eyes covered, and yelled between the irrational sobs, "Oh my GOD! I don't know why I can't stop crying."

I wanted to punch him with my foot mainly because I wanted to be the one on the ground pitching a fit about the waterworks.

We were on what became the last date when we ran into a friend of his. After introductions, his friend said to me, "You had me fooled for a minute! I thought you were his ex-wife. Holy crap—you look just like her."

There it was: unclaimed baggage.

I put him behind the rope stanchions and dusted off the extra, empty chair once again.

BAGGAGE-FREE CHEESECAKE

(White Chocolate Cheesecake Tart with Peaches and Lavender)

INGREDIENTS:

Crust

- 1½ cups graham crackers
- ½ cup walnuts
- ¼ cup sugar
- ½ cup butter, melted

Cheesecake

- 2 (8 oz) packages cream cheese
- ¼ cup of sugar
- 2 T lemon juice
- ¼ cup sour cream
- 2 large eggs
- 1 tsp vanilla extract
- 6 (1 oz) white chocolate baking bars, melted

Topping

- 3 ripe peaches cut into ¼" wedges
- ½ cup of lingonberry jelly
- ½ tsp cornstarch
- Water
- Edible lavender flowers

DIRECTIONS:

Preheat oven to 350° F. Grease the bottom and sides of a 13" × 9" pan. For the crust, place the walnuts and graham crackers into a food processor and pulse until they are crumbs. Transfer to a bowl. Add sugar and butter.

Combine until the mixture holds together. Press the mixture into the bottom of the pan. Bake at 350° for 10 minutes. Set aside to cool.

In a small bowl, melt white chocolate by placing it in the microwave for 15-second intervals, stirring in between each interval. Once it is melted completely, set aside.

In a large bowl, beat cream cheese and sugar until creamy. Add sour cream and melted chocolate. Mix well. Scrape down sides of mixing bowl to ensure even mixing. Add vanilla and lemon. Lastly, beat in the eggs one at a time, only until blended. Pour cheesecake into pan. Place in 350° oven and bake for 30 minutes.

In a saucepan, combine jelly and 1 cup of water and bring to a boil. Add cornstarch. Stir. Add peaches. Place peaches on cheesecake and pour the remaining jelly over peaches. Chill and serve. Garnish with edible lavender flowers.

II.

CHEESECAKE CAN HOLD ITSELF TOGETHER NO MATTER WHAT

Not all dates are bad. If they were, our species would have either died out long ago or mastered asexual reproduction by now. Some dates go well in and of themselves, and some dates lead to more serious relationships, which is nice. Some relationships tie the knot whereas others unravel. Time tests the tether.

In the tangled thread of dates gone well, a relationship sort of stumbled into being. There were a lot of awkward moments in the beginning, which later became the charming fallibility of our story.

One weekend in winter, my boyfriend and I went to the Northwoods Region of Wisconsin, which is beautiful. Wisconsin in winter is very still. It is frozen and, occasionally, the sun shines. On this particular sunny day, a walk across a small, frozen, inland lake shone a light on destiny's picture of our togetherness.

After his early morning run to the local grocery store for what he claimed were the best apple fritters in the world, we stuffed our gullets and headed out. We slowly made our way across the lake, bellies full of sugar, because in northern Wisconsin, in winter, our only other option for entertainment was day drinking. The sky was clear, the air brisk, and the morning was beautiful despite the bitterness of winter's cold.

Before us was a mile long, black-and-white expanse of snow and frozen water.

A frozen lake makes slow, low, eerie noises as the ice expands and contracts with the fluctuating heat of the day and cool of the night. The inland lakes call out from within the ice a song similar to mating whales. It is hauntingly beautiful.

Regardless of the ice's moan, by midwinter it is typically thick enough to tow a shanty behind a truck to the middle of the lake. That day, a quick glance around the lake provided evidence via a dozen or so shanties that the ice was indeed thick enough for the two of us. Despite the indicia, the guy was still leery about walking across the middle of the lake for fear he'd fall through. He misconstrued his self-admiration as having weight. We ventured out anyway.

With the sun in full swing, the ice was a highly dramatic opera. We had been walking and talking for a while, crossing back across the lake toward home when it happened. We were just past the middle.

Feeling comfortable, warm, and safe in the relationship, I let the spirit of my prank-loving grandma come out. Keeping in step, I threw up my arms, yelped, and folded at the knees, pretending to fall through the ice.

In a panic, he yelled, "Oh F*ck!"

He simultaneously pushed me out of his way, using me as a launching pad, and ran in the opposite direction. Kneeling on the ice, I laughed so hard I almost peed fritters.

Then I realized what just happened.

Let's review: He thought I was falling through the ice. Instead of trying to save me, he pushed me aside and ran away. He didn't stop to help. He didn't reach for me to try to hold me up. He didn't hold himself firmly together. He panicked and ran.

It was only funny until it wasn't. There it was. The oracle had spoken.

I'd never thought about myself as a damsel in distress who needed rescuing, but I also never thought of myself as being left to die by a boyfriend who saves himself first, foremost, and only. The hero of any story is the one who can hold himself together and runs *to* versus *away* from where he is needed. There was no hero in this story, just a bad prank and a sad realization.

The chill of that weekend's experience settled in deeper than the winter snow, which naturally took me back to warming thoughts of cheesecake. Cheesecake holds itself together. It sticks with you. And although it may not earn the title of hero/heroine, cheesecake is exactly what you need to thaw even the coldest of realizations.

THE LAUNCHING PAD

(Apple-Spice Cheesecake with Shortbread Crust and Cinnamon Glaze)

INGREDIENTS:

Crust

- 1 cup all-purpose flour
- 1 cup almonds
- ¼ cup sugar
- ½ cup cold butter, cut into pieces
- 2 egg yolks
- 1 tsp vanilla extract

Cheesecake

- 4 (8 oz) packages cream cheese, room temperature
- ⅔ cup sugar
- ¼ tsp salt
- ¼ tsp cardamom
- ½ tsp cinnamon
- ¼ tsp ginger
- ½ tsp vanilla extract
- ¼ cup plain yogurt
- ¼ cup apple butter
- 3 eggs, room temperature

Apple topping

- 5–7 medium-sized red baking apples
- 2 T sugar
- Pinch of salt
- ¼ tsp cinnamon
- Lemon juice

Glaze
- 1 cup powdered sugar
- ½ tsp cinnamon
- 4 T water

DIRECTIONS:

Preheat oven to 325° F. Grease the bottom and sides of a 9" springform pan. In a food processor, combine almonds and flour. Pulse until they are crumbs. Add sugar and butter. Pulse until they are crumbs. Transfer to a bowl. Add broken egg yolks and vanilla. Stir until combined. Press the mixture into the bottom and sides of the springform pan. Bake for 14 minutes. Remove from heat. In a small bowl, beat egg whites until frothy. Using a pastry brush, coat the shortbread crust with egg white. Bake for 5 minutes. Set aside to cool.

Wrap the pan in a double layer of aluminum foil, and place in a large baking pan to prepare for the water bath.

Wash and dry apples. Cut in half (top to bottom) and cut in half again (side to side). Remove core. Using a mandoline set to #2 setting, slice apples. Place apples in a bowl with cold water and squeeze with lemon to prevent browning. Remove the apple slices and dry them. Set them aside.

In a large bowl, beat the cream cheese and sugar until smooth. Add the salt and spices. Combine. Add the yogurt and apple butter, beating until smooth. Add eggs, one at a time, and mix until combined. Add vanilla. Mix. Pour over prepared crust.

Starting on the outside edge of the springform pan, place the apples, flat-cut side to the center, around the perimeter, overlapping each apple by half of the other apple. Continue to place the apples in this manner, working concentrically in toward the center of the pie. Make sure the last few apples are sliced very thin so they can be rolled up into a cylinder and placed as the center of the flower. Sprinkle with salt, cinnamon, and sugar mixture.

Bake at 325° for 55–65 minutes. The cheesecake will jiggle in the middle but remain firm around the edges when it is done. Turn off the oven and let the cheesecake remain in the warm oven for 30 minutes. Remove cheesecake and cool to room temperature.

To create the glaze, combine powdered sugar and cinnamon in a bowl. Add water until it is smooth and pourable. Drizzle over apples. Refrigerate until ready to serve.

Using a serrated knife, gently cut across the top of the apples before cutting the cheesecake. The serrated knife will help to minimize the apples moving while being sliced.

12.

CHEESECAKE IS ALWAYS COMPLIMENTARY

Once upon a time I spent what felt like my kid's college tuition on matching, sexy-sexy, lacy, and bedazzled undergarments for a weekend away with my boyfriend. A set in black, another in red, and two sets in pink, I was prepared for whatever the mood conjured up. Let me save you some money and effort: don't waste your paycheck on lacy bras and panties. Men aren't looking. The only time a man is paying attention to your underwear is when your bra fastens in the front … and even then, his attention is not on what you were trying to wow him with, rather on how to hoist the mantrap over your head.

Just stick with the comfy cotton briefs and send your kid to college.

Women know how much effort goes into our look before we even think about putting a foot over the threshold to the scrutinizing world outside. We do more than just a shower and apply an aftershave. We spend millions of dollars on products, hours on applications, and even more on choosing the right outfit and shoes so that we specifically invoke more than, "You look alright" from anyone's lips. We already do that to ourselves. The mirror-mirror-on-the-wall is constantly pointing out our flaws and telling us that the fairest in the land is someone else. We step out of our house seeking to prove the mirror wrong. We are looking for the jaw drop though most nights I'd settle for a double take and a smile.

I dated someone with a skill for flattery that tended to be more grease fire in the kitchen than coq au vin flambés at the dinner table. No amount of effort on my end ever led to speechlessness on his. Try as I may.

Around the time of the fancy undies, I had intentionally assembled an outfit in which standing, and standing very still at that, was my only option. We all know those pants. The only way to get them on is through acrobatics and sucking it in while laying down for a gravity assist. Perched like a teeter-totter board at the end of my bed, unable to bend down and help my feet into shoes, I slid into the highest, sexiest, ankle breakers I had, and then tried my best to finish getting ready without breaking a sweat or letting go of my breath. Sheer shirt, smoky eyes, and hair ironed straight, I was *en pointe* for a "Da-yum!" It took me more time to get ready than I ended up spending out that evening.

I drove to my boyfriend's place while holding vigil for both my zipper and for no sudden movements while driving. "Please, Lord, don't let my high heel wedge underneath the gas pedal."

Feeling gorgeous, I was caught between wanting a slight breeze so I could get air into my lungs without inhaling and knowing that the slight breeze might also blow me off the precarious balance of those shoes.

He saw me coming, outwardly confident and looking for the big win in the game of nice words and compliments.

A kiss hello. A hand on my back, he said, "Hey ... I like your shirt." *Swoon*.

The homage to flattery fell flat again.

I knew compliments were possible because I heard him talk about his mamma. I'd witnessed praise during well-played games on NFL Sundays, overheard banter about the brilliance of *The Office*.

I couldn't compete with his love of Pearl Jam or an apple fritter. That being said, it would have been nice to hear something more flattering than what he just said about his new beer can koozie.

He said he liked my shirt—it was as underwhelming of a sentiment as when he commented on the expensive undies that were being tossed aside like they were found roadside near a cheap motel.

"Yup. Nice," he'd said. The bikini wax, mani-pedi, and smoky eye shadow never even got an honorable mention ... much less appreciation.

Expressions of admiration shouldn't resemble soup spills down the side of the stove. The right kind of adulation boomerangs the good stuff right back. The wrong kind has me donning the grannie panties and reaching for a pint of ice cream.

Cheesecake is always complimentary. It brings the meal to its crest; providing an apogee of flavor that leaves everyone feeling good about their culinary experience and even begging for an encore. That's flattery. That type of sweet talk will get you more cheesecake.

DA-YUM GOOD CHEESECAKE
(Ginger Cheesecake with Grapefruit and Mint)

INGREDIENTS:

Crust
- 1 (8 oz) bag of crispy gingersnap cookies (about 2 cups)
- 4 T butter, melted

Cheesecake
- 1 (4 oz) package goat cheese
- 3 (8 oz) packages cream cheese
- ½ cup Greek yogurt
- ⅓ cup sugar
- ½ cup honey
- 1 T ginger powder
- 2 tsp freshly grated ginger
- 3 whole eggs
- 1 egg yolk
- 1 T cornstarch

Topping
- 3 red grapefruits
- Whipped topping
- Mint leaves

DIRECTIONS:

Preheat oven to 350° F. Prepare an 8" springform pan by coating with butter. Place a round of parchment paper on the bottom of the pan. Wrap the pan in a double layer of aluminum foil. In a food processor, pulse the cookies until they are crumbs. Transfer crumbs to a bowl. Add the butter and combine until the mixture holds together. Press the mixture into the bottom and sides of the springform pan. Bake for 10 minutes. Set aside to cool.

Place the springform pan in a large baking pan to prepare for the water bath.

In a large bowl, beat goat cheese and cream cheese together until smooth. Add yogurt and beat. Add sugar and honey. Beat until creamy. Add powdered ginger and fresh ginger. Beat until smooth. Add eggs, one at a time, and blend until combined. Pour over crust. Add approximately 1" of water to large baking pan to create water bath. Carefully place pan in oven and bake for 50–60 minutes. Turn off oven and let cheesecake sit in warm oven for half an hour. Remove cheesecake and cool to room temperature (about 2 hours).

Increase oven temperature to 400° F. With a sharp knife, cut away grapefruit peel to expose the pulp. Carefully remove each section of the grapefruit by cutting the membranes away. With larger segments, cut in half so each segment is approximately ¼" wide. Place on parchment paper on a baking sheet. Bake for 20 minutes. Cool on a cheesecloth towel. Keep on towel until cheesecake is cool. Arrange slices of grapefruit, starting at the outer edge of the cake moving toward the center, to create a circular rose pattern. Garnish with whipped cream and mint leaves.

13.

CHEESECAKE NEVER HAS
TO SAY IT'S SORRY

There are many things we can be sorry about: bangs, neon, shoulder pads, wall-to-wall shag, Thomas Kinkade giclée prints, cussing in front of small children, forgetting a birthday, overcooking the turkey, and the like. Cheesecake is not one of them. No apologies are needed in the making of a cheesecake nor in the sharing of one.

"I'm sorry I gave you a piece of cheesecake," said no one ever, and it is never followed by, "I'm sorry I ate that."

There might be some regrets around the fat content of a cheesecake, but anyone eating a cheesecake will know that is the penance paid for such bliss.

We've all done things for which we've been guilt-ridden or compunctious. Generally, we are fallible; filled with flub; bungling about, spilling our inaccuracies, assumptions, and misconceptions all over the place like beer from plastic cups at a college house party.

"Sorry I was late."

"Sorry about the wine glass."

"Sorry ... I don't get it ..."

I've apologized for plenty thus far and I'm certain I will have more retractions and pardons to beg later. The key is to not repeat the things for which you need to make amends nor to continue accepting redress for reruns, either. Atone, learn, grow, and move on.

It was a beautiful summer afternoon; a perfect day to get married. My girlfriend wore a simple summer dress and her husband-to-be, linen. Their yard, set with tent, lights, caterers and music, looked like something out of a movie as they prepared for the parade of family and friends for this occasion. I was a bucket of tears and a wad of used tissue. Happiness brings on my waterworks and envy makes my nose run.

Like so many other times, I came to this event as a party of one, unencumbered, unattached, and with the job of being the social butterfly—floating from guest to guest with polite conversation and laughter as easy as the breeze. No one asked this of me nor have those descriptors ever been uttered when I show up in my full personality. I took it on as a vocation, called to add spice to otherwise bland interactions amongst couples long together and hungry for novelty. This reframing of what could otherwise be called a lack of filter or filling a void or attention seeking puts a positive spin on the Universe's divine plan to keep me single. I can hide behind redescription like a fawn in the forest.

The bride grabbed my elbow. "Hey—you need to talk to someone over here."

She pulled me to the steps of the stone patio and introduced me to the only other single person at the wedding, a friend of the groom.

He stood about two inches shorter than I and the slick of his hair piqued my affinity for car crashes. It was a little too shiny to mean anything good. All the same, duty called, and I kicked us off with some polite banter about the weather and did not touch the gleam on his head to see if it was Brylcreem soft or Suave stiff.

A few minutes later, when the weather lost its zeal in conversation, his phone rang. He was sorry, but he had to take the call and he walked away.

It was hard to tease out if I was more offended at his obvious lack of interest in me or the fact that he was answering his cell phone at a wedding.

The undeniable setup disguised as a random happening wasn't going the way the bride had intended. She returned with her matron of honor in tow for research. They gauged my apathy and hypothesized that was too quick to judge, making excuses around his business tenor. Another couple intervened on my behalf, stating that the man looked "greasy." The groom overheard and came to the defense of his friend. Soon the wedding's focus shifted into debate as to whether this would be a match or not. The man, who had since returned, offered to take me out to lunch so we could come to our own conclusions.

Hopeful, I sat at a small table outside a café, sipping iced tea in the summer sun. The sounds of the city, alive with the ebb and flow of activity, were as calming and comforting as the rhythm of ocean waves, sloshing against the sand. A horn honked, jarring me into focus. My date, who was late, leaned toward the passenger side, yelling to me that he was just looking for a place to park. At the table, he apologized, but "things had come up." He ordered tea and placed his phone on the table, signaling that his interest would only be held until the phone pinged. It did and he apologized again. He had to take the call.

In between calls and apologies, he tried his best to explain that he owns a business and that its success often interrupts his ability to be social. I shrugged and said, "That's a choice you make."

He was already off with another call.

Our date happened in ten-minute fragments between twenty-minute calls. The ring of the phone splintered stories and left sentences dangling with annoyance more so than suspense. He pleaded for a do-over when he wasn't so busy.

The lack of polish in his punctuality coupled with his inattentiveness left me feeling like we were trying to ignite the sparks of relationship using damp matches and a candle without a wick. Though regrettably and sadly familiar with the feeling, the eternal optimism of deep-rooted codependency encouraged me to let go of how late he was and hang on to the idea that he arrived at all.

With a second date having fared the same as the first, I pulled the plug on the third … but we had it anyway.

My diminishing enthusiasm for this guy was still not equal to or greater than the desire to not be alone. I imagined myself surrounded by forgiveness for him like white light or like sparkles in a glitter globe, as we tried again for lunch. The visualization went dark when the date was late again. I felt like I could have been replaced by a reservation and a numbered placard because my role was to hold the table until he graced it with his presence. His emphasis on his own eminence was exacerbated by the insincerity of his amends, and I wasn't having it. Apology after apology. Sorry. Sorry. Sorry. Three dates in a row of the same: Late; Sorry. Parking; Sorry. Phone; Sorry, sorry, and sorrier. I asked him if he ever grew tired of apologizing so much. It seemed he lived a very sorry life.

Without apology and with some indignation, I used his sorriness to let me off his hook. Sorry—not interested. I deserve better than late and a lot more than nothing. It may have taken me three tries to get there, but at least no one could say I judged him too quickly or that I didn't give him a chance. I'm only sorry I gave him three.

Cheesecake is never sorry. It's always on time. It always delivers uninterrupted pleasure. It is unapologetically sweet, remorseless in its decadence, and unbending in flavor. It has nothing to be sorry about other than, maybe, the empty plate.

AN UNAPOLOGETIC CHEESECAKE

(Rosewater and Cardamom Cheesecake)

INGREDIENTS:

Crust
- 1 sleeve (9) graham crackers
- 1 cup almonds
- ⅓ cup sugar
- 2 T all-purpose flour
- ½ cup butter, melted

Cheesecake
- 4 (8 oz) packages cream cheese, room temperature
- ¼ cup heavy cream
- ¼ cup sour cream
- ¾ cup sugar
- Pinch of salt
- 2 tsp vanilla extract
- 1 tsp cardamom
- 1 tsp vodka
- 2 T rosewater
- 4 large eggs plus 2 yolks, room temperature
- 2 T cornstarch

Topping
- ¼ cup strawberry jam
- 2 T rosewater
- Edible rose petals for garnish

DIRECTIONS:

Preheat oven to 350° F. Grease the bottom and sides of a 9" springform pan with butter. Wrap the exterior of the pan in aluminum foil, and place in a large baking pan to prepare for the water bath.

Set aside.

In a food processor, pulse the almonds until they are crumbs. Add graham crackers. Pulse until they are crumbs. In a bowl, combine crumbs, flour, sugar, and butter. Combine until the mixture holds together. Press the mixture into the bottom and sides of the springform pan. Bake at 350° for 8 minutes. Set aside to cool.

In a large bowl, beat the cream cheese until smooth. Scrape down the sides of the bowl often. Add cream and sour cream and blend until smooth. Add sugar, vanilla, cardamom, rosewater, and vodka, beating until fully combined. Scrape the sides of the bowl often. Add eggs and yolks, one at a time, beating well after each addition. Add in the cornstarch and beat until combined. Pour filling into the prepared pan.

Add approximately 1" of water to large baking pan to create water bath. Carefully place the pan in the oven and bake for 60–75 minutes. Edges should be firm with center still jiggly. Turn the oven off and let the cheesecake sit, undisturbed, for 30 minutes inside the oven with the door shut.

Remove the cheesecake from the oven and run a knife around the inside edge of the cake to release it from the pan. Place the cheesecake (still in the pan) on a wire rack and cool to room temperature. Loosely cover and refrigerate for at least 8 hours.

In a saucepan, heat jam and rosewater until melted and liquid. Pour over top of cheesecake. Garnish with edible rose petals.

14.

CHEESECAKE IS GOOD FOR YOU
BY BEING BAD FOR YOU

Running in heels. Eating jelly-filled donuts while driving to an interview. Owning a pair of haircutting scissors. Butter. DIY electrical repairs. Deciding you remember how to skateboard when you're over forty. Sick leave, an open credit card, and Amazon Prime. 10× magnified lighted mirrors. Forever21 when you're not. The phrases, "How hard can it be?" and "Sure, why not," and "What's the worst that could happen," and "What should I do with these extra screws?" We know what's bad for us.

Awareness, however, and the ability to do something about it, or something else at all, is like trying to *not* scratch the poison ivy you picked up either culling wildflowers illegally from the nature trail or weeding along the fence line by your neighbor's unkempt lawn. Not scratching the itch feels like insanity. Scratching the itch begets immediate pain and more itch. It's hell.

The bad boy, the rebel, and the lone wolf have tripped my switches so many times that my brain seems to have given up trying to direct my affections elsewhere. The itch is that I know he's the wrong guy. My friends tell me he's wrong. However, if he broods, count me in. If he has a motorcycle and rides it like he means it, check, and scratch.

If he's indignant, irascible, and a challenge to make smile, consider the panties floor fodder. All the lady parts come alive when the wrong guy saunters into pheromone-sniffing range. I recognize what will become the fast-and-furious passion-play-to-heartbreak the instant my brain registers that the bits and tits have sprung into action and my mind mumbles, "This guy is an asshole. I can tell already."

That's the first clue that the game is on, that it's rigged, and that I am going to look back on this later and shake my head for falling for it again.

The draw is the hardened edge and the challenge is to soften it; to be the one special person who can fix him, heal him, love him, and receive his love in return. His appeal is in the confidence it takes to not give a f*ck because so many women, just like me, give too many. We hand them out like candy on Halloween to everyone who comes knocking because someone out there, some sugar-hungry, love-starved man is going to say that my bonbons are enough.

Bad-boy addiction begins early. I can trace mine all the way back to fourth grade when a new boy came to class. He was a year older than the rest of us, had actual biceps, and wore a hefty scowl as his everyday play face. On his first day of school, he wore *jeans* and didn't choose anyone to show him around. Having been held back, he was one big, angry fourth grader. The girls in the class lit up like fireflies on a hot and humid summer night, flitting around him as though he was a mason jar. It was a country school, but this kid came out of nowhere and he didn't follow any of the rules written or otherwise. Our collective self-respect didn't stand a chance against the boy who would yell, "Leave me the hell alone!"

Even in fourth grade, we girls were acutely unaware but bustling for his affections so we could fix him. That poor boy didn't get left alone until high school when the bad-boy pool grew exponentially larger. Some girls went soft and decided to like the athletes. Not me. I tied myself to the track of every emotional train wreck heading my way, subconsciously hoping to be rescued from myself.

The high-school brooders turned into college cankers, who then grew up to become irksome men; each just as mysteriously appealing as the next. It was as though the emotionally unavailable man held the allure of bacon.

We are aware of the signs we choose to overlook. We can't tell how he feels about us. We don't know if we are in a relationship or not. Compliments are "C" grade or lower. Plans are never made more than a week out and there is no talk about future anything other than his eventual retirement. He doesn't look you in the eye and gently trace the hair away from your face. There may be passion but there's a distinct lack of intimacy. It always feels like something is missing and I've come to learn that it's him. Unavailable is unavailable.

Dating the bad boy is like eating bacon hoping to improve your cholesterol rating. Some things are just bad for you.

Very few things can boast about being bad while also being good for you, but cheesecake can. It's hardwired into our brains that things like fats, sweets, and chocolate make us feel better. The brain gives us a little boost of dopamine when we have things like cheesecake. It literally makes us happy. After a hard day at work, a breakup, or shopping for swimsuits, cheesecake takes the edge off, making everything a little softer and a little sweeter. Our brains tell us this is true, and our bodies agree. That little bit of decadence is so good for us, and it is readily available when we want it.

I want things that are good for me. I want to love and be loved. A husband? A dog? A baby? Or maybe just another slice of cheesecake.

I don't want a badass. I wanted a nicer ass.

BADASS BLACKBERRY
(Lavender Blackberry Cheesecake with Rosemary)

INGREDIENTS:

Crust
- 2 cups graham cracker crumbs
- 1 cup almonds
- ⅓ cup sugar
- ½ cup butter, melted
- Pinch of salt

Cheesecake
- 3 (8 oz) packages cream cheese
- ½ cup sugar
- ⅓ cup honey
- ½ cup sour cream
- ⅓ cup lavender blackberry sauce (below)
- 3 T cornstarch
- ½ tsp lavender extract
- ½ tsp vanilla extract
- 3 eggs, room temperature
- 1 cup fresh blackberries, cut in half

Lavender blackberry sauce
- 1 ripe plum
- 1 cup blackberries
- ¾ cup red wine
- ⅓ cup sugar
- 3 T fresh rosemary
- 3 T fresh lavender

- 1 T lemon juice
- 1 T cornstarch
- Pinches of salt and cracked pepper

Topping
- ½ cup blackberry sauce
- 1 tsp cornstarch
- ¼ cup water

DIRECTIONS:

Preheat oven to 350° F. Grease bottom and sides of a 9" springform pan. For the crust, place the graham crackers and nuts in a food processor and pulse until they are crumbs. Transfer to a bowl. Add sugar, salt, and butter. Combine until the mixture holds together. Press the mixture into the bottom and sides of the springform pan. Bake for 8 minutes. Set aside to cool. Wrap the pan in double layer of aluminum foil, and place in a large baking pan to prepare for the water bath.

To make the blackberry sauce, cut plum into quarters. Remove pit. Place plum, blackberries, rosemary, lavender, and wine into a blender and puree. Transfer to a sauté pan and bring to a simmer. Add sugar and lemon juice. Simmer for about 6 minutes to soften plums and reduce wine. Remove from heat and strain over a bowl, using a spoon to push the softened plum through the strainer. Discard the plum meat, skin, and seeds. Add a pinch of salt and a pinch of black pepper. Stir. Set blackberry sauce aside until ready to use.

In a small bowl, combine ½ cup of blackberry sauce and halved blackberries. Stir and set aside.

In a large bowl, beat cream cheese and sugar until smooth. Add honey and sour cream. Beat until smooth, scraping down the sides often to ensure even mixing. Add ⅓ cup blackberry sauce and beat again. Add cornstarch. Mix well. Add vanilla and lavender extracts. Mix well. Beat in eggs, one at a time, until fully combined.

Pour half of the cheesecake batter into the prepared pan. Carefully spoon blackberries in sauce on top of layer. Cover with remaining batter. Add approximately 1" water to a large baking pan to prepare for the water bath. Bake cheesecake for 60–75 minutes or until sides are firm and the center jiggles. Turn off oven and let cheesecake cool for half an hour in the oven. Remove from oven and cool to room temperature (2 hours).

In a small saucepan, heat blackberry sauce, water, and cornstarch until thick. Pour over cheesecake.

Refrigerate until ready to serve.

15.

ADDING ALCOHOL TO CHEESECAKE WILL NOT MAKE IT AN A**HOLE

I admit it. I'm a woo-girl. It only takes one cocktail for the old high school cheerleader to return, clapping, jumping, and just having a good time. I love everybody when I'm buzzed. Hugs all around. It's not really the alcohol, but that certainly doesn't hurt the volume of my jubilee. Two cocktails and I'm looking for someone to hold my hair back.

Booze and my body have always had a tumultuous relationship, so I tiptoe around imbibing like the baby's sleeping. I still love everybody and can be a bit of fun, but I spend a lot less time with my face being where it shouldn't.

Sometimes, with my feet on the railing of my back deck, overlooking the mudslide I call a backyard and listening to the birds, I enjoy a glass of wine. Some say that drinking alone is an issue. I'd say the bigger issue is my lack of landscaping. The two things are not related.

I spend a lot of time thinking about my landscaping because thinking about dating feels like more work than hauling dirt. The breaks between dates have grown longer as I contemplate the repetitive nature of my choices and what is wrong with my picker or my persona.

Over the years, I convinced myself that I had learned and grown out of bad relationships in the same way I outgrew shoes as a child.

Then I remembered how I'd intentionally wreck the cheap shoes my mom would get for me because secretly I wanted better ones.

That is also eerily accurate to many of my relationships. "No," "No thank you," and shaking my head have all become part of my growth vernacular.

No is a powerful word. No to dates. No to setups. No to going out alone. No wallowing. No self-pity. No time for bullshit. No. No. No.

This wasn't depression. It was focus. I was done dipping my toes into the icy waters of relationships that didn't pan out. I was done swimming in the sludge.

My daughter, however, pushed me back into the water. One day she said, "You know, Mom, sometimes you have to say yes, too."

She was talking about saying yes to her, but I knew that her mind saw the bigger picture. Even though I told her "No, I don't," I knew she was right.

When I met the dog trainer I said yes. I said yes to seeing if he was trainable.

In a crowded and bustling restaurant, I met my date at the bar. He waved me over with a chin tilt, holding up a glass that was rapidly being emptied. The hostess immediately motioned to seat us, and my date threw back the last of his drink.

As first dates go, this one was starting out average and benign. Nothing really jumped out during the question-and-answer portion. The conversation was expectedly awkward as we navigated through stories that hopefully made us sound more interesting than we actually were. We ordered appetizers and drinks; a martini for him and a red wine for me. Over the course of dinner and dessert, which took about an hour and a half, he lined up five more martinis, slamming each one down as if it were slightly annoying. I nursed the one glass of wine as if it was sacred. If I learned anything in college, it was that nobody is interested in the girl who drunk vomits in the shrubbery.

I was trying not to count the drinks, but the conversation, which was awkward already, degraded a bit with each emptied glass.

He had done well in his life and did more than just train dogs. The dogs he trained were *champions* and he traveled the world because of them. This led to his world-class farmstead which wasn't just a typical farm, but an apparent fifty-acre trophy case for prized roosters, bulls and cows, a horse or two, a couple of kids, a hefty staff, and, of course, the dogs. His prized possession was his own sustainability on the farm, which felt admirable. He referred to it as the "best way to live."

I began to wonder in hearing his lists of the best of the best, all things world-class, A-class, choicest of the choices, is there room for someone like me who likes simpler things like my mediocre coffee pot that makes unfabulously okay coffee? Was there a participation prize for being average? I couldn't decipher if he was setting me up for a competition or if he was trying to impress me with how perfect my life could be if we made it to the award ceremony.

Parting ways at the end of the dinner, he wished the date didn't have to end as he grabbed my shoulders, holding himself steady, and moved his face toward my face for a kiss. Dodging the slobber with my sobriety in check and a ninja move to boot, he got a cheek. I offered to call a ride for him, and he declined, reminding me that he's a big guy and that alcohol doesn't impact him. He got behind the wheel of his brand new, MotorTrend award-winning, two-thousand-pound instrument of mobile destruction and drove home. I was relieved to live in the opposite direction.

A week passed and I assumed that after a cocktail and five martinis, he didn't even remember going on a date. It was a comfortable yet disturbing thought … until he reached out to me for date number two. A glass half-full kind of optimist, I agreed, although reluctantly.

Another restaurant left me hopeful that the red flag from date one was a figment of my imagination. A kiss on the cheek to say hello dashed that hope. He was already at least one drink in. Unsolicited, he let me know that he had come from a very important meeting, the kind in which a fine scotch is served to seal the deal or something like that. I gave a nod like meetings I attended, which were never, also included a fine scotch.

Everything about date number two was a repeat performance of date number one, including the conversation. He had no recollection. I did my best to navigate around the boozy blabber, watching the glasses line up again. Like before, he slammed the drinks down as though they tasted bad, and he was forced to do it. He looked miffed when each new drink arrived like it was another damn chore to do, and I wondered why he was so irritated, especially since he was ordering the drinks of his own accord. It was a silent question because although there was plenty of talking happening, very little of it was from me. My words, much like his questions about me or what my interests might be, were still in the stall, waiting to be let out. What he did set free were his opinions about my drinking water and what he thought I should be drinking to loosen up a bit. He really didn't like it when I ordered a water for him. That's when the belligerence showed up. He blew like moonshine mash after a lightning strike, spewing accusations: I was crazy just like the last woman he dated. I was like his ex-wife: an idiot. I was like his mother, always monitoring him. He was right and I was wrong. *He* didn't have a problem, he said. I did.

All I could think was, "My God, man, it was just a glass of water!"

Another date, another washout. Someone clearly missed the "good citizen" part of his training. He was supposed to be wooing me with words of kindness not barking insults. I did what good trainers do: I did not reward the excessive noise, rather, I walked away from it.

Another week passed and I was grateful for the sweet canine at my side and the silent phone on the table. However, before long, the dog trainer reached out again, boasting a great time on our second date, and inquiring about a third.

He was the *Bad Santa* of dog trainers, and no one needs to be reminded about how poorly sequels to bad movies go. Teetotalling a glass of wine on the deck again, and again alone, I said no. It felt good. It felt as gratifying as seeing the potential of my backyard while appreciating the work that had already been done.

When it comes to cooking, alcohol enhances the flavor of what is already there. Adding a little bit of bourbon to your blueberry crumble pops the subtle flavor of those berries: Vodka to your vanilla cake and it will practically sing happy birthday to itself. Charge up your cheesecake with a bit of brandy to brighten its often-subtle tone. Likewise, when it comes to people, adding alcohol emphasizes that individual's innate character. If an asshole is already there, adding alcohol will make it bigger and more obvious.

Fortunately, there are no asshole cheesecakes.

THE DRUNKARD
(Brown Sugar and Bourbon Cheesecake)

INGREDIENTS:

Crust
- 2 cups graham cracker crumbs
- 1 cup pecans
- ⅓ cup brown sugar
- ½ cup butter, melted
- Pinch of salt

Cheesecake
- 3 (8 oz packages) cream cheese, room temperature
- 1 stick (8 T) butter, room temperature
- ½ cup brown sugar, packed
- ½ cup granulated sugar
- ¼ tsp salt
- 3 eggs plus 1 yolk, room temperature
- 2 tsp vanilla extract
- ¼ cup heavy cream
- ¼ cup bourbon

Topping
- 1 cup brown sugar, packed
- ¼ cup corn syrup
- ½ cup heavy cream
- 4 T butter
- ¼ cup bourbon
- 1 tsp vanilla extract

DIRECTIONS:

Preheat oven to 350° F. Grease bottom and sides of a 9" springform pan. In a food processor, place nuts and graham crackers, pulsing until they are crumbs. Add sugar and mix. Transfer to a bowl. Add butter and combine until the mixture holds together. Press the mixture into the bottom and sides of the springform pan. Bake for 8 minutes. Set aside to cool. Wrap the pan in a double layer of aluminum foil, and place it in a large baking pan. Set aside.

In a large bowl, beat the cream cheese until smooth. Add butter, brown sugar, white sugar, and salt, and beat until light and fluffy. Add eggs and yolk, incorporating one egg at a time and mixing until smooth. Add heavy cream, bourbon, and vanilla, and beat until combined. Pour batter into the prepared pan. Fill the large baking pan with 1" hot water. Bake cheesecake at 350° for 60–75 minutes. Cheesecake will be stable along the edges but still jiggly in the middle.

In a small saucepan, melt butter with brown sugar and corn syrup. Bring to a boil. Remove from heat and add cream, vanilla, and bourbon. Stir quickly. Add pecans and simmer mixture on low for 10 minutes. Set aside.

When cheesecake has baked for 60–75 minutes, remove from oven. Carefully place pecans in caramel on top of the cheesecake and pour remaining caramel sauce on top. Bake for 10 minutes. Turn off oven and let cheesecake rest in a warm oven for 30 minutes. Remove from oven and cool to room temperature. Run a knife along the inside edge of the pan to release the cheesecake and prevent cracking. Refrigerate at least 6 hours or until ready to serve.

16.

CHEESECAKE DOESN'T HAVE TO GET BAKED TO BE A HIT AT A PARTY

After a while, one grows accustomed to being single. There is a lot of autonomy in it. My house is set up with just my stuff and it rarely is in disarray. I don't wonder where things disappear to, like a hammer, because I'm the only one who uses them, and I put them back. I didn't have to have a conversation about how adopting a dog would impact the both of us when I spontaneously went to the humane society for a pet. I didn't have to explain why it made sense to drive two hours one way for a stray cat who needed a home. No one leaves the seat up. And no one's snoring keeps me up at night. The perks are plentiful.

It isn't all roses and champagne in this party of one. Loneliness is real. Lifting heavy things involves phone calls and begging. Walking my dog when I have the flu is just as bad as having to make my own soup while I'm sick, too. No one is making dinner when I work late. Then again, no one is messing up my kitchen, either. It's about balance.

It is around the time that I comfortably settle into singleness once again, that one of my coupled friends will find someone with whom they want to couple me up. My resistance is almost a reflex at this point. I become suddenly unwilling to trade my Hula-Hoop, roller skates, and a little plastic pool for a bigger TV and a set of his-and-her matching pajamas. I huff and puff about how much I love "me" time and how great it is to have weekends alone, untethered and unbothered by a need to grill out. I even rename these isolating experiences as "writer's retreats" knowing full well I'm just scrolling through TikTok for hours on end.

The intentions are good, though they get couched in denial, too.

"It's not a setup," they said. "We would never do that."

And yet, there he was: Mr. Not-a-Setup sitting next to me like he was just pulled out of a magician's hat or something. He just happened to appear at a concert we all attended, and he happened to magically be age appropriate, single, and apparently looking for love. He leaned in for conversation during the concert. Maybe it was flirting. Maybe it was informative. I will never know because I was listening to the band. His low, gravely, voice came with a scent of sage and patchouli. It wasn't sage but it took me a while to figure out that he was high. His seat was often empty.

He bought me a CD and wrote, "Awesome concert!" on it, along with his phone number, a charming gesture and one noted for the books.

The ringing in my ears from the concert had long gone away before we ventured out for a first official date.

Two steps past his doorway and he presented me with a large bowl of Doritos swallowing a smaller bowl of ranch dressing. He loved to cook, he said. He exclaimed that he was out to win me over with this awesome dynamic duo of flavors, missing the fact that Frito-Lay had developed this flavor combo well over a decade ago. His fascination with his invention of Doritos and ranch dressing together competed with his pride over the pinball machine in the living room, the wall-sized television blasting a Tom Petty concert, and the old-school record player belting out some Fleetwood Mac. It reminded me of being fifteen. I was fascinated, a bit entertained, and wondered out loud if he drove a Camaro.

The familiar scents of something smoked, a bit of patchouli, and cover-up mouthwash hung in the air.

Randomly, he'd step outside for things he said he forgot in his car, none of which arrived in the house. Each trip made him a little more glassy-eyed, and a little stronger in the wafting. He fiddled with the volume on the television and the record player, putting the two bands in a decibel competition. I suddenly felt old and wanted him to turn that racket down. He didn't have a kerchief up his sleeve like a magician, but he had a way of wizardry that messed with my age.

Underwhelmed and overstimulated on many fronts, I suggested we leave … more than once. He said it was an awesome idea. The upside of going on a date with a stoner is that he said I was hilarious almost every time he looked at me. I wasn't.

At a casual dinner party with friends, the jaunts outside continued. He was so high that his vocabulary found the skip in the record, putting his one-and-a-half-word repertoire on repeat. Language was the only moderation he showed. I tried making excuses, but there was little I could say that could make bringing the "Yup. Awesome" guy on a date any less fodder for gossip.

At evening's end, he announced an awesome time and invited me in with the promise of the remaining chips and dressing. The lure of leftover junk food, not surprisingly, was not quite enough to get me over the threshold one last time.

The magic of the evening had gone up in smoke and no bowl of Doritos and ranch dressing could rescue the bunny that clearly needed to go back in the hat.

YUP, AWESOME CHEESECAKE

(White-Chocolate Lemon-Lime Non-Bake Cheesecake)

INGREDIENTS:

Crust

- 1½ cups graham crackers
- 1 cup almonds
- 1 T lime zest and 1 T lemon zest
- ½ cup sugar
- ½ cup butter, melted

Cheesecake

- 1 package (or 8 sheets) gelatin
- 1 cup lime juice
- 2 (8 oz) package cream cheese, room temperature
- ½ cup sugar
- 1 (14 oz) can sweetened condensed milk
- 1 cup of white chocolate, melted
- 3 T lime zest
- 1 cup heavy whipped cream, whipped to peaks

Topping

- 1 cup lemon curd

DIRECTIONS:

For the crust, place the graham crackers, nuts, sugar, and lime/lemon zest in a food processor and process until they are crumbs. Transfer to a bowl. Add butter and combine until mixture holds together. Press the mixture into the bottom and sides of a 9" springform pan. Freeze for 30 minutes.

In a small bowl, heat lime juice in a microwave until tepid. Add gelatin. Stir until dissolved. Set aside.

In a large bowl, beat the cream cheese and sugar until smooth. Add the condensed milk. Blend. Add the melted white chocolate. Blend. Add lime zest and lime gelatin. Blend. Fold in whipped cream and mix until combined. Pour into the prepared pan and refrigerate.

Warm lemon curd for about 20 seconds in a microwave. Pour on top of cheesecake and smooth.

Chill overnight and until ready to serve.

17.

CHEESECAKE MAY BE HEALING
BUT IT DOESN'T CLAIM TO
BE A MIRACLE WORKER

I swear I met Jesus in a wine bar. He wore cowboy boots and walked around like he was the waft of warm bread, enticing people in like mom's comfort food. And the way he moved was like spreading butter on that bread. He put at least one "mmm" in "mmmm, mmmm, mmm."

The guy walked over to me by parting the sea of random others, intent upon an introduction. This was the first and only person, who, at the moment of meeting, left me speechless. I couldn't help but to stare. Restating his name, he shook the unintentionally listless lettuce leaf of my hand. I heard nothing but what I thought was the sound of my lady parts purring.

I wanted to leave immediately to find the nearest confessional, but there was a naked woman sprawled on the floor before us. We stared at her. We weren't the only ones. Everyone was taking a good, long look.

It was a figure-drawing class and the man with the long, wavy, brown hair and the white linen shirt was an engineer who liked to sketch.

Our paths crossed again a few days later—this time, all people were fully clothed.

Turned out, the man was in pursuit of my holy grail. He chased and wooed and worked the game. The dinner dates were elaborately planned and often expensive. The gifts were embarrassingly numerous. Like so many other women, I melted in a relationship so intense with activity. We became almost inseparable in a very short amount of time.

We hiked the back side of a mountain where the landscape was free of trails and other humans. He found a sturdy stick to support his walk, long hair flowing past his browned shoulders, the light of day behind him creating a sort of halo. He assured me that he knew the way. Through the poison ivy and snakes, over the rapids and slippery rocks of the river whose course we were following, we passaged. The destination, he said, was a beautiful and remote waterfall. It was going to take my breath away and "was right around this bend," he said. Many bends and six miles later, as the sun began to set, we reached our heavenly harbor.

The only remote part of the waterfall was the path that we took to reach it. We could have taken the road traveled by all the other tourists to the area as this was a popular state park. By the time of our arrival at the falls, dark had set in, we were miles upriver, and we needed a ride from a park ranger back to his van.

For him, he professed that it was about the journey. The sojourn connected us to nature, he said. I appreciated his sense of adventure and agreed that it was a day well spent but suggested that maybe next time we visit the state park from the visitor's entrance.

The relationship was a course in continuous adventures.

In the heat of a Southern summer night, on another passage to God-knows-where, I loaded his van with an overnight bag and some extra granola bars. Our dates were typically undefined, held at least one surprise, and included at least one catechetical lesson that left me wondering if his looks were intentionally crafted.

For once, our time together didn't leave me wishing I had paid better attention to *Survivor*. We had just gone out for a simple night on the town with some friends. There was no extraneous feat and no experiential bible study. That is, until someone wandered off. I didn't think much of his wandering. Wandering happens. He'd done it before. He always returned. This time, however, a lot of time passed. When he didn't come back to tend to the flock, I set out, like so many others, on a search for my savior.

He was quickly located in the back part of the venue, hair down, hands out, eyes closed and healing people. He literally had his hands cupped over someone's head inaudibly mumbling something that was probably supposed to be a prayer. I tapped him on the arm and asked if he was okay. He didn't respond. Healing, it seemed, needed his undivided attention. There were two other people lined up behind the person who was being revivified.

I squatted down to look into the face of the person being ministered to and I said, "You know he's not actually Jesus, right?"

From my squat, I looked at the makeshift messiah. He was not in his best frame of mind. By the look he gave me, you'd have thought I'd slapped his mother. He dropped his hands from the inflicted, stood up straight, and gave me a glare that made me feel like a lamb in the lion's den. The scampers scattered. From his mouth flew a string of explicative insults aimed at whom he must have perceived as his Judas: me. He stormed off, cursing and yelling and flailing his arms wildly overhead. Back at his vehicle, the tantrum continued. He threw my stuff out of it, got behind the wheel, turned the key, and drove off. He continued to curse me out and gesture wildly as he left me curbside in a town twenty miles away from home. This was not a very Jesus-y thing to do. It was one in the morning.

Although the pretend prince of peace disappeared, three days later, he stepped out from behind the rock. This time he came during the night and threw the detritus of our relationship onto my driveway.

An encounter with this level of crazy is like taking a lovely, mindful stroll at dusk and a random bat swoops out of nowhere and entangles in your hair. It came as a surprise and scared the shit out of me. Dude was off his rocker.

Typically, "unbalanced" shows up pretty quickly and is quite obvious, but sometimes, like this, it was well hidden behind a respectable day job and a Crest-white smile.

It got me to thinking about Ruth, from college. We shared many conversations about nun-dom, and I began to wonder if she was right. As much as my independence had served me well in this pursuit of a better life, maybe my love would be better spent serving God instead of man. I contemplated the nunnery. I just didn't want to wind up dating another whack-a-doo behind an everyday Joe mask. I thought about becoming a monk.

I landed in the kitchen. It reminded me to find the metaphors and to seek solace in my springform pan. The imposter missed the cheesecake mark by a long shot and when the structure of who he pretended to be was removed, he was just a goddamned mess.

Cheesecake, on the other hand, which is genuinely heavenly through and through, and may lead to shout-outs to the Almighty, will never come out of the pan as sauerkraut. Cheesecake soothes your soul. It tastes like a prayer answered. Cheesecake does not profess to work miracles, rather, it allows you to experience the divine simply by being itself.

A SLICE OF HEAVEN
(Stout Caramel Non-Bake Cheesecake)

INGREDIENTS:

Crust
- 2 cups graham crackers
- 1 cup pecans
- ¾ cup sugar
- ½ cup butter, melted

Cheesecake
- 2½ (8 oz) packages cream cheese, room temperature
- ⅓ cup stout caramel (plus ¼ cup more for whipping cream) (recipe below)
- 1 cup heavy whipping cream
- ½ cup powdered sugar
- 1 package gelatin
- ½ cup sugar
- 1 cup boiling water
- 2 T cornstarch
- 1 tsp vanilla extract

Stout caramel
- 1 cup stout beer
- ½ cup butter
- 1 cup brown sugar
- 2 T corn syrup
- 1 tsp vanilla extract
- ½ cup heavy cream

Chocolate ganache
- ½ cup chocolate chips
- ¼ cup heavy whipping cream

DIRECTIONS:

Grease bottom and sides of an 8" springform pan. For crust, place graham crackers and pecans into a food processor and pulse until they are crumbs. Add sugar. Pulse until blended. Transfer to a bowl. Add butter. Combine until the mixture holds together. Press the mixture into the bottom and sides of the springform pan. Set aside.

In a small saucepan, heat beer and butter until boiling. Lower heat to medium-high and reduce beer and butter for 8–10 minutes or until it looks opaque and a bit like gravy. Add sugar and corn syrup. Bring back to boiling and cook for about 8–10 minutes more until it coats a spoon. Remove from heat. Stir in vanilla and cream. Bring back to a boil, stirring constantly, for 2–5 minutes until it thickly coats the back of the spoon. [Caramel sauce can be tested for stages by having a clear glass of cool tap water and pouring drops of syrup into the water. If the syrup looks like flakes sinking to the bottom, the syrup is done. If it enters the soft-ball stage (where it remains a ball at the bottom of the glass but is squishy when touched), remove from heat and add ¼ cup more cream. If it enters the hard-ball stage, it has been cooked too long.] Set aside.

In a chilled mixing bowl, whisk heavy cream until stiff peaks form. Add powdered sugar and caramel and whip until combined and still peaking. Place in a bowl and set aside.

In a small bowl, mix sugar and package of gelatin. Add 1 cup of boiling water and stir until blended. Set aside.

In a mixing bowl, beat cream cheese with ⅓ cup caramel until smooth. Add gelatin mixture, ¼ cup at a time until well blended. Add vanilla and cornstarch. Fold in whipped cream mixture and combine until well blended. Pour over crust.

Use the extra caramel and pour lines over the top of the cheesecake. With the warm ganache, also add lines over the cheesecake. Using a butter knife, swirl the chocolate and caramel toppings into a pattern on top of the cheesecake, incorporating some into the cheesecake. Set in the refrigerator and chill overnight or at least 6 hours before serving.

18.

CHEESECAKE CAN STOP AN ARGUMENT, NOT START ONE

The ancient Greeks used to say that "love is a madness." They said that it was dangerous, as well as foolish, to engage in. True fact. Having been married before, I must agree.

To say that we argued a lot in our marriage would be a gross overexaggeration and an insult to the silent treatments we perfected over the years. We stewed. We held grudges. We had arguments upon occasion.

Such occasions were typically on days when we woke up. Other occasions included times when we were together and times when we were apart.

To argue is to present the evidence for or against a thing, but argu-ING turns the presentation of evidence into a shouting match. I like to believe that I calmly present evidence when an opportunity arises. I also like to believe that my consumption of cheese staves off osteoporosis and that sugar is a necessary component, like bacon, to a well-balanced diet.

I believe that sometimes there are too many cooks in the kitchen. Sometimes there are too many spoons stirring the pot. I believe that sometimes arguments happen, and that sometimes the piehole of the arguer just needs something stuffed into it.

When I was married, my husband and I quibbled about really dumb things. We bickered about the placement of the litter box. I asserted that it did not belong in the kitchen, and he contended that the cat wouldn't be able to find it otherwise. One of us was wrong and it wasn't me.

We argued about whether to paint the bedroom ceiling and trim all in the same deep forest green to match the walls. After he insisted that I was wrong to vote a big, fat "no" because it would feel ominous and depressing, he painted the room the way he wanted anyway and then complained that the room felt ominous and depressing.

One spring, about a year into the marriage, I noticed that our front porch had some soft wood near the steps. I suggested that we look into quotes to get the wood replaced. He didn't think it was to that point, so we waited. Summer splintered the edges and by fall I was using the side entrance to the house. Clearly, the wood was rotten, but he didn't agree. I measured the deck to his dismay and used winter to gather information about the "when and how" of deck replacement. He insisted that I was overexaggerating and complained of being tired of spending money on my whims. Another spring, another argument.

I wondered what it would take for him to see that the front porch was beyond our combined obstinance and had reached the point of being an actual threat. He set out to prove me wrong, storming out the front door and jumping up and down with great vigor on the deck. Once. By the second landing, he had crashed through. Argument over.

I certainly wasn't right about everything. I textured the bathroom ceiling because it would hide the cracks, not knowing I had just created opportunities for mold colonies to prosper. I also didn't know that rats would love my compost pile by the alleyway or that leaving a window open for fresh air while we traveled would create an escape route for the cats who took the week we were away as an opportunity to fill our living room with birds and bird parts. I could be wrong. It was just rarely that we had to argue about that.

We bandied about whether to put beans in the chili, how many nights a week we should eat pizza, what to name the dog, and what to name our child. If we weren't disagreeing over something, it probably meant that one of us was sleeping. We hashed over that, too.

Our arguments were proof that we lacked negotiation skills, an ability to cooperate, and were unable to communicate with each other in general. He bought me a book on communicating in relationships, clearly telling me that he thought I was the problem. I communicated my thoughts clearly by chucking the book across the room. I could accept being self-deprecating enough to back down from disagreements, but I would not accept blame. I had my limits. Eventually, our lack of cooperation and failure to communicate landed us in a courtroom, using lawyers to speak on our behalf in regard to our divorce.

Being right or wrong was only on the surface of our indignations. Beneath the noise were our bigger issues that neither one of us could admit to yet: the childhood wounds that battened us to bad behaviors on a repeat loop called codependency. We didn't see it that way, though. Even if we did, we probably would have fought about it.

We also argued about cheesecake, especially my evidence that cheesecake is better than just about anything—including men.

I let the evidence speak for itself.

Love isn't madness. It's knowing when to cram some cheesecake into that piehole of yours and just nod in agreement because you know I'm right.

THE EVIDENCE

(Pear and Elderflower Cheesecake)

INGREDIENTS

Crust

- 2 cups graham cracker crumbs
- 1 cup almonds
- ⅓ cup sugar
- ½ cup butter, melted
- Pinch of salt

Cheesecake

- 3½ (8 oz) packages cream cheese
- ½ cup pear sauce (see below)
- ¾ cup sugar
- ½ cup sour cream
- 2 T cornstarch
- 3 T elderflower syrup
- 3 eggs plus one yolk
- 1 tsp vanilla extract
- Pinch of salt

*Pear Sauce

- 1 large, ripe pear
- 1 cup water
- ¼ cup elderflower syrup
- 1 tsp cornstarch

Topping

- 1 pear, sliced thin

DIRECTIONS

Preheat oven to 350° F. Grease bottom and sides of a 9" springform pan. For the crust, place the graham crackers and nuts in a food processor and pulse until they are crumbs. Transfer to a bowl. Add sugar, salt, and butter. Combine until the mixture holds together. Press the mixture into the bottom and sides of the springform pan. Bake for 8 minutes. Let cool. Wrap the pan in a double layer of aluminum foil, and place in a large baking pan to prepare for the water bath. Set aside.

To make the pear sauce, cut pear into quarters. Remove seeds. Place pears, water, and syrup, into a blender and puree. Transfer to a sauté pan and bring to a simmer. Simmer for about 6 minutes to soften the pears and reduce liquid. Remove from heat and using a mesh strainer, push the liquids and softened solids through the strainer into a bowl. Discard the pear meat and skin. Return sauce to pan and add cornstarch. Simmer until thick like gravy. Remove from heat and set aside.

In a large bowl, beat cream cheese and sugar until smooth. Add ¾ cup of pear sauce and beat again. Add sour cream and mix until well blended, scraping down the sides often to ensure even mixing. Add eggs, one at a time and blend until combined. Add cornstarch. Mix well. Add vanilla, pinch of salt, and elderflower syrup. Mix well. Pour over crust. Fill larger baking pan with 1" hot water.

Cut pear (for topping) in half. Using a mandoline, thinly slice the pear and place on top of the cheesecake.

Bake cheesecake at 350° for 55–65 minutes. Cheesecake will be stable along the edges but still jiggly in the center. Pour remaining pear sauce over top of cheesecake and return cheesecake to oven. Bake for 10 minutes more. Turn off oven and let cheesecake sit in warm oven for half an hour. Remove from oven and cool to room temperature (2 hours) Refrigerate overnight (about 8 hours) or until ready to serve.

19.

CHEESECAKE MIGHT WRECK YOUR DIET, BUT IT WON'T WRECK ANYTHING ELSE

They say that getting too comfortable in a relationship is one way to wreck it. I can think of at least a dozen more ways.

Sometimes relationships turn on themselves like a rabid rodent to its next of kin. Sometimes relationships end because they never should have started in the first place. In the case of my marriage, it was a combination of both.

"What are you trying to do—kill me?" my husband pushed his dinner of acorn squash aside.

"Yes," I responded. "A slow and unsuspecting death through vegetables."

He fed the deadly dinner to the dog.

"Fred likes the squash," he said. The dog eating the squash wasn't a matter of taste. It was a matter of breed. Fred was a beagle, and he ate everything.

Elbows on the table, my face against the fold of my knuckles, I took a few deep breaths. Things were not going so well. Marriage, it seemed, was harder than I thought.

To be fair, it was challenging for both of us, and we put in our best effort to pretend to want to fix it. The therapist we saw gave us homework that we chose to ignore, each citing the other as the one who didn't do the work. Blame was as comfortable to wear as an old bathrobe. Culpability was a worn pair of house slippers. Accustomed to discontent, the vow "until death do us part" no longer felt like a promise. Instead, it loomed overhead like an oncoming threat.

Before anyone called a bluff, I filed for divorce.

As challenging as marriage was, divorce was just plain ugly. Divorce, it turns out, like most breakups, does not bring out a person's best behaviors. Anyone who has gone through a divorce knows this all too well and wonders, like I did, how we both managed to come out of it alive.

So much felt overwhelming and devastating.

Entering splitsville doubled the household expenses while cutting the income in half. It took the wind out of the sails of savings; halting progress toward *someday* promises, island vacations, and ridiculously priced shoes. My financial security was reduced to the change jar on the shelf in the kitchen.

The empty chair returned, and it had a scarlet letter "D" on it. Divorced and dateless were synonymous. They were the new black and I wore it everywhere.

Friendships desisted for any number of reasons: his versus mine, religious dogma, socioeconomic differences, and rumor. As tough as it was, the natural selection of support systems in the wake of a separation made the stronger friendships fortify and deepen and the lesser ones fade away. It took a while for that to sink in, though. Initially, all I felt was the goose in the duck-duck game, chasing after my reputation as a good person and trying to catch and hang on to whatever allies I could. What I lost in quantity, I gained in quality. The steel girders of girlfriends became unshakeable through all the storms and quakes of those times, and they have become my foundation for everything ahead.

The most crushing blow of the disunion came in the destruction of happily ever after.

The expectations of how I thought life was supposed to be went up in a raging house fire. The dreams that had begun to cement my steps of probability in a fourth-grade game of MASH-up met with the mushroom cloud of nuclear destruction as the ink dried on the divorce papers. Letting go of *forever* broke my heart more than leaving behind the husband. Recalculating expectations meant doing my math on my fingers instead of an algebraic graphing calculator. I had to simplify everything for the sake of sanity.

The marriage felt like skinny jeans at 7 p.m. on Thanksgiving. Its demise was an uncinched belt. Even though it felt like it wrecked who I thought I was supposed to be and my role in the future I only dreamt about, eventually, I traded the skinny jeans for sweats, and made room by clearing out what was no longer beneficial. I reached for a second slice of cheesecake because I was about to embark on a future that was wide open with possibilities.

THE CALM AFTER THE STORM
(Earl Grey Cheesecake with Lemon Cream)

INGREDIENTS:

Crust
- 1½ cups graham cracker crumbs
- 1 cup walnuts, toasted and cooled
- ⅔ cup sugar
- ½ cup butter, melted

Cheesecake
- 3 (8 oz) packages cream cheese, room temperature
- 1 cup sugar
- 1 tsp ground Earl Grey tea, ground into a fine powder
- ½ cup sour cream
- ½ tsp vanilla extract
- 3 eggs
- ½ cup half-and-half simmered with 2 Earl Grey tea bags
- 2 T cornstarch

Topping
- Juice from ½ lemon
- ½ cup sour cream
- 2 T sugar
- 2 T lemon curd (can be purchased in a grocery story)

DIRECTIONS:

In a small saucepan, bring half-and-half to a simmer and add 2 Earl Grey tea bags. Remove from heat and allow to steep for 10 minutes. Remove tea bags.

Preheat oven to 350°. Grease bottom and sides of a 9" springform pan. In a food processor, combine graham crackers, walnuts, and sugar. Process until they are crumbs. Add butter and combine until the mixture holds together. Press into the bottom and sides of the springform pan. Bake for 8 minutes. Set aside to cool.

Once cool, wrap the pan in a double layer of aluminum foil, and place in a large baking pan to prepare for the water bath.

In a large bowl, beat the cream cheese until smooth. Add sugar, sour cream, and tea mixture. Beat until smooth. Add powdered tea and mix. Add cornstarch. Beat. Add eggs, one at a time and beat until combined. Add vanilla. Mix until blended.

Pour batter into prepared springform pan. Add 1" hot water to the baking pan and bake cheesecake for 60–75 minutes. Edges of cheesecake will be stable, and center will be jiggly.

In a small bowl, mix ½ cup sour cream with lemon, lemon curd, and sugar. Pour over cheesecake and bake for 10 minutes. Turn off oven and let cheesecake cool in oven for half an hour. Remove from oven and cool to room temperature (2 hours). Run a knife along the inside edge of the pan to release the cheesecake and prevent cracking. Refrigerate cheesecake (still in pan) for 6 hours or overnight.

Remove from pan and serve.

20.

CHEESECAKE ALWAYS MAKES
YOU FEEL BETTER

We know what makes us feel better: new shoes, best friends, cheese-cakes, and grandmas.

My grandmother survived cancer before surviving cancer was a thing; she was blind in one eye, had heart disease, and was diabetic. She was often at odds with her body and encountered such with a bit of sass, weekly bowling, and baked goods. With all she'd been through, she knew how sweetness was just the right medicine for some of life's most bitter moments.

As a kid, bitter moments meant school was *not* cancelled due to snow or worse, that Halloween was. Grandma always had a candy dish on hand just in case.

Being the first one out in dodgeball or the last one picked for the team ranked almost as high on the bitter-moment scale as finding out on Monday there was a birthday party over the weekend that you weren't invited to. A slice of cake for the one I missed could cure almost any need-to-feel-better moment around.

The biting rancor of adulting, however, meant grabbing a deck of cards and a handful of nickels and heading over to grandma's house for her fantastically wayward advice doled out between losing hands of gin rummy, diminishing coins, and her sweet, sweet cheesecake.

Heartbreak was a common topic. She heard about my summer crushes, the challenges of kissing with braces, and how being flat chested left me last to be picked again and again.

My grandmother passed away in 2001. I have needed her more than a few times since.

One such moment had me gathering girlfriends in droves to meet the collective comfort of one, long-since-gone, grannie. It may have been a Tuesday. I'm not sure. Certainty, paired with my composure, escaped the hen house and flew away knowing full well that the sky just caved in.

Parity, like sitting on a teeter-totter, can throw you when one person jumps off. One person moves on while the other person is supposed to pine for all of eternity. The imbalance, I'm certain, falls under a rule of physics or some such thing.

This story started as my first online dating debacle. With just a few days on the site, I had five different winks from five different men, which led to four phone conversations and four no's. The fifth shut down his page.

Convinced that online dating was really shopping for serial killers and unwilling to be the next female found in a swamp somewhere, I shut down my page. A few weeks later, under the influence of wine and two girlfriends, the collective we, wobbly and giggly, reopened my page to have a look-see and a few laughs. Amongst the potbellied athletic types, the couch potato adventurers, and men whose photos belied their age by decades (not in their favor), was number five. He resurfaced: Another wink, another request for a phone call, and another no from me. He lived 120 miles away.

I said no, but the wine gave him my number anyway.

Phone calls led to long-distance traveling, which led to almost a year of falling madly in love. I had found my match. Our kids liked each other. My dog liked his cat. There was little that we felt could ever come between us … except the road. Regardless of the closeness we felt, distance became our undoing. I couldn't move. He couldn't move.

We were at an impasse. With no way to make the miles shorter, I was eventually forced to call the time of death for the relationship, and he agreed. It was a very sad time, and I surrounded myself with every comfort that I could: friends, booze, and bad advice.

Moving on was challenging and slow, but I was making steady work of it. I accepted the setups and tried to say yes more than no. Comparison turned my efforts to quicksand and I was sinking fast. Some relationships were harder to let go of than others.

Stillness, I had decided, would be my best bet.

Alone on a Saturday night, nestled on my couch with a good book and a fire in the fireplace, my phone rang. Number five. Over a full year had passed since we closed the cold-storage door on our potential future together.

Not more than a word after hello and we confessed that this had been a miserable year. The conversation was easy and unending. For much of the night, the phone held the only space that distance could not take away. He arrived a weekend or so later, and it was like he had never left.

The span of time did nothing to dissuade what we felt, though the spread of our horizon was still insurmountable. Again. We tried to remeasure the miles in possibilities as the weeks passed and again, we fell short. Gridlocked a second time, we let our brains make a decision that was in direct opposition to our hearts, but we knew, that ultimately, this was the correct choice. We said good-bye for the second time.

Sporadically, texts and calls were exchanged but they became shorter and further apart. Months later, the communication had once again gone silent … only to resurface in almost mirrored timing. This time, however, we couldn't connect. Literally. Voicemail recorded remnants of stories in short, frayed pieces, back and forth, without much being said.

One night, maybe it was a Tuesday, I got through. He didn't have time to talk but he didn't want to miss my call, he said.

"How are you?" he asked.

"I'm well. You sound busy."

"Yeah. I am. I've been trying to call you. I was hoping to talk to you …"

"Sorry. Sometimes life … you know …"

"Yeah. Say—I'm actually running out the door. I have a plane to catch. Going to Mexico … sort of a vacation. I'll be back in two weeks. Can I call you then?"

"Mexico! Sort of a vacation? What's a 'sort of' vacation? Are you going there for work?"

"No," he said. "My honeymoon."

He kept talking as he put the luggage in his vehicle, explaining everything. I heard absolutely nothing. I may have started to dial for help—beep beep beep-beepbeepbeepbeep—right over his voice. I don't know how long he talked or how many numbers I pushed while he talked. It's all irrelevant to the fact that one of us had moved on and it wasn't me.

I cried for days. Maybe weeks. It could have been a month or three or six. Who knows? Everything was a blur. I gathered the girlfriends along with my emotional equilibrium before heading off, once again to the pantry to sort through my stuff and figure it out. This bitter moment was going to be sweetened the way grandma would have done it. I set out a deck of cards next to the completed cheesecake and a photo of grandma. Cutting us each a slice, I pulled out two forks and told her all about it.

MY GRANDMOTHER'S CHEESECAKE
(Non-Bake Cherry Cheesecake)

INGREDIENTS:

Crust
- 1½ cups of graham crackers
- ½ cup walnuts
- ½ cup sugar
- 1 cup melted butter

Cheesecake
- 2 (8 oz) packages cream cheese, room temperature
- 2 cups of powdered sugar
- 2 pints of whipped topping (such as Cool-Whip)
- 1 tsp vanilla extract

Topping
- 1 can of cherry pie filling

DIRECTIONS:

For the crust, place the graham crackers and walnuts into a food processor and pulse until they are crumbs. Transfer to a bowl and add the sugar and the melted butter. Combine until it holds together. Press mixture into the bottom of a 13" × 9" pan. Set aside.

In a large bowl, beat cream cheese and sugar until creamy. Add whipped cream and vanilla. Spoon over crust and smooth with an offset spatula or knife. Pour cherry topping on top. Chill until ready to serve.

21.

CHEESECAKE WILL NEVER ASK YOU IF IT'S THE BEST YOU'VE EVER HAD

You know someone asked.

I have been asked. Many girlfriends had someone ask and, yet none of us have ever asked the question in return. There would be no way to prepare for an answer that you don't want to hear.

After a night of intimacy, my friend's boyfriend asked her if he was the best she'd ever had. When I asked her how she responded, she said, "Well, I hesitated. That was the first mistake." She continued, "and then I said, 'We sure are good together.'"

The pause and the tangential answer prompted him to ask how she felt about his sexual abilities. How was his performance? He wanted to know. He wanted reassurance and she couldn't give it to him. He looked for his confidence in what he had hoped would be a reciprocal statement. He said to her, "Well—you are the best *I've* had." And then he kept talking about how great she was and kept asking if she thought he was great, too. With each consequent statement, she said he became a little more, how do we say ... factual. She was a saint to put up with his insecurity.

I can't say that I wouldn't have told him to put a sock in it.

Basically, if a man has to ask, then he has to know that the answer is no. Anything other than "no" is just being polite. And for the love of all that's sacred between the sheets, he needs to stop fishing for his ego in the empty space of an "O" that didn't happen.

If I'm asked if he is the best I've ever had, he should know that I have had plenty of time to come up with a response over the years and the conversation is going to end up like this:

"Am I the best you've ever had?"

"No. Do you want to know who is? Because I still have his number, and I'm sure he'd give you some tips or something."

"Am I the best you've ever had?"

"No. You are like #7 or so."

"Am I the best you've ever had?"

"No. But you are not the worst. Let me tell you about *that* guy …"

The "am I the best" question is usually followed sometime later by "where did you learn that?"

We can safely assume that I've been rehearsing those answers as well.

Here's the thing: cheesecake doesn't put you on the spot like that. Cheesecake doesn't ask if it's the best. It doesn't need to.

Let's say, for argument's sake, that it was not the best. Let's just say that the last cheesecake you had was slightly better. The current cheesecake isn't going to compare itself to the last cheesecake or to any other cheesecakes. It isn't going to wonder if its flavor was good enough for you. It isn't going to wonder if the last cheesecake was a 9" cheesecake and compare it to its 8" size.

No. Cheesecake is just cheesecake. It knows it's satisfying. It knows it's smooth, and it knows it hits the spot. Every time.

There is confidence in cheesecake, and we all know that confidence is the real aphrodisiac. It's not arrogant like mousse quenelles or insecure like green Jell-O with fruit in it. Cheesecake is firm without being strict, sweet without being saccharine, and bold without being brazen.

Cheesecake never needs you to lift up its ego, it only wants you to lift up a fork and enjoy.

THE BEST CHEESECAKE
YOU'VE EVER HAD

(Red Velvet Cheesecake with Tart Cherry and Wine Compote and Chocolate Ganache)

INGREDIENTS:

Crust
- ¾ cup walnuts
- ¼ cup black walnuts
- 1½ cups chocolate wafer cookies
- ½ cup graham crackers
- ⅓ cup sugar
- ½ cup butter

Cheesecake
- 3 (8 oz) packages cream cheese, room temperature
- ¾ cup sugar
- ½ cup cherry jam
- 3 T cocoa powder
- 1 cup sour cream, room temperature
- ¼ cup buttermilk
- 2 tsp vinegar
- 3 eggs plus 1 yolk, room temperature
- 1 tsp vanilla extract
- ½ tsp red food coloring

Cherry topping
- ½ cup cherry jam
- 1 T sugar
- ½ cup tart cherries, pitted and halved

- ½ cup red wine
- Dash of salt
- 1 T cornstarch
- ½ cup walnuts, ground to crumbs

Chocolate topping
- 1 (3½ oz) bar of dark chocolate
- ⅓ cup heavy cream

DIRECTIONS:

Preheat oven to 350° F. Grease sides and bottom of an 8" springform pan. In a food processor, pulse the walnuts, black walnuts, and wafers until they are crumbs. Add sugar. Pulse until blended. Transfer to a bowl. Add melted butter and mix until crumbs hold together. Press the mixture into the bottom and sides of the springform pan. Bake for 8 minutes. Set aside to cool. Wrap the pan in a double layer of aluminum foil, and place in a large baking pan to prepare for the water bath.

In a small bowl, combine cocoa powder, vinegar, buttermilk, and sour cream. Mix until well combined and set aside.

In a large bowl, beat the cream cheese and the sugar until smooth. Add jam. Beat until smooth, scraping sides of bowl often. Add cocoa mixture to cream cheese mixture. Blend. Incorporate eggs and yolk, one at a time and mix on low. Add vanilla and food coloring and mix until blended. Pour over prepared crust.

Add hot water to baking pan so it reaches about 1" up the side of the spring-form pan. Place in oven and bake at 350° for 60–75 minutes. Cheesecake is done when sides are stable, and center is still jiggly. Turn off oven and let cheesecake sit in warm oven for 30 minutes. Remove from oven and cool to room temperature (about 2 hours). Run a knife along edge to release from pan and prevent cracking.

In a saucepan, combine cherries, cherry jam, wine, and sugar. Bring to a boil. Reduce heat to simmer and add cornstarch to thicken. Cool mixture. While still warm, place topping on the cheesecake.

Cool. Add crumbled walnuts to topping. Cool completely.

Chop chocolate bar into small pieces. Place in a small bowl. In a separate bowl, heat heavy cream in a microwave (approximately 45 seconds) until hot. Pour over chocolate. Let sit for 1 minute. Mix until chocolate is completely melted. If more heat is needed to melt chocolate, place bowl over another bowl with hot water in it. When chocolate is melted, pour over cherry topping. Smooth with offset knife. Refrigerate until ready to serve.

22.

CHEESECAKE IS NEVER DONE
IN JUST FIVE MINUTES

It seems like I could just stop there. Drop the mic. Boom. Enough said. End of book.

*

Just like size, duration matters. And if I were more succinct in my stories, that would be it. But I'm not, so the five-minute thing is going to take its dear sweet time in reaching its peak and then quietly, slowly, softly wrap itself up in the denouement and drift off to sweet sleep.

Five minutes can be a time warp depending on the situation. Five minutes is agonizing when waiting for that return text message. Five minutes is not long enough when you're getting texts from someone you are not interested in. Five minutes provokes anxiety when meeting your date that many minutes late. Five minutes is exhausting when running and five minutes is not always enough when your heart is racing for all the right reasons.

It's that last reason, the not enough, that I am going to metaphorically explore by way of dessert.

Cheesecake, even the so-called instant kind, is never done in just five minutes. It takes fifteen minutes. It says so on the box.

There are only two ways to have a cheesecake done in under five minutes. One way is to buy it premade and the other is to mix up some cream cheese with some powdered sugar and put it on a graham cracker. It's not really cheesecake, but it's as close to done in five minutes as cheesecake is going to get.

Recipes vary in the time required to make your cheesecake, and it is good to know what to expect on the front of the recipe versus being surprised at the end with an unfinished cheesecake. The only thing that can be done with an unfinished cheesecake is toss it out and start again from scratch another time.

And for the love of keeping the so-called oven hot, don't ask if it's done and then try to pick up where you left off. It takes the steam out. Trust me. Reheating the oven to cook it again is just setting yourself up for disappointment. Undone is done that isn't.

It's at that point that one can take matters into one's own hands and put some damn cream cheese and sugar on a graham cracker and call it a night.

For any variety of reasons, sometimes the rush of five minutes can be enough for both parties involved. And into that *sometimes* satisfying five minutes went careful preparation of all the right things to make the lady sing an opera aria. The prep time, if included, could be hours or days in the making. The prep time, for the *sometimes* satisfying five minutes, leads to a lingering cooldown period that could also last hours or days if one is lucky. For the UNsatisfying five minutes, it's like eating one potato chip.

Sometimes, the right amount of prep time seems to be there. But sometimes, the oven hasn't been turned on to preheat. Worse, still, is when it was turned on, but dessert wasn't given enough time to bake, and no one ends up getting dessert. Like so many other women I know, I have had this experience. Don't have us miss out on dessert. We love dessert. We look forward to dessert.

My tall, dark, and handsome loved grocery shopping, so to speak. We had walks, talks, outings, dinners, movies, us time, and group time. We had good times together and enough time apart to make the time together feel special. The relationship seemed to be going very well and was taking its time, as relationships should. Eventually, we made it into the proverbial kitchen for some good ol' baking.

The relationship, a culmination of all the right ingredients, had a LONG prep time and I was looking forward to a dessert that would be over the moon once the oven was hot enough. Believe me when I say, it was hot enough. The oven had been on preheat for EVER.

Wrapped and ready for the oven, the batter hit the floor. Nothing got cooking. His approach was enough to ding his own timer. He was done and I was left wondering what the hell he was so happy about.

In a shocking move, he said, "That was amazing," and a hand went aloft looking for another hand to complete the high five.

I interrupted his winning moment by asking, "You're kidding! You know there are two people involved in this, right??"

There is no amazing if only one person gets a prize. It was the beginning of the end. We could follow the recipe, mix the ingredients, and *double* wrap the pan, but we never made it to dessert.

I found myself searching the pantry for graham crackers far too often.

No matter how simple the recipe or how well the ingredients are mixed, a good cheesecake is never done in just five minutes. And if you are putting cream cheese and sugar on a graham cracker, I get it. I'm sorry.

All good things take time, including cheesecake.

THE DESPERATE MEASURE
(Instant Cheesecake)

INGREDIENTS
- Graham crackers
- 4 oz cream cheese, room temperature
- ½ cup powdered sugar
- ½ cup sour cream
- ¼ tsp vanilla extract

DIRECTIONS:

In a small bowl, whip cream cheese until smooth. Add sugar, sour cream, and vanilla. Beat until well mixed. Place in an airtight container and store in the refrigerator until needed.

When needed, remove from refrigerator. Open graham crackers. Dip crackers into cream cheese mixture.

I've been there. Feel better soon.

23.

CHEESECAKE IS ALWAYS SATISFYING

Taking a sledgehammer to a wall in my kitchen was satisfying. Cleaning up the mess from construction for the next six months was not.

Hearing the sound of my neighbor, who is a concert violinist, rehearse for her next concert is satisfying. Listening to the sounds of the beginner lessons she provides to support her career as a concert violinist is not.

Having a man slowly and tenderly study the curves of your body with his hands as though any pressure would lift the beauty from your skin is satisfying. Having a man use his hands during intimate moments as though he dropped his toll change between the seat and console of his car where it slides just out of reach, is not.

My good friend is a sex expert. I have no idea whether this is a certification or a self-proclamation. What I do know is that she knows a lot more than I do about things I never thought that I ever wanted to know. She informed me that some men don't really know what they're doing when it comes to a woman's satisfaction. All too aware of this already, I leaned in for more.

She said that the problem stems from the fact that neither men nor women want to know or understand women's anatomy beyond the basics of the general parts. She offered to instruct me as to the sensitive nature of any number of my personal parts, and asked me to de-pant, undies and all. I politely declined, letting her know that I was pretty sure I knew where I was sensitive and had my parts well under control.

My friend, with all good intention of wanting to help me help men, asked me to talk her through the process of ringing my own bell. She said it was important that I become comfortable talking about this so that I could teach an intimate partner how to satisfy me. She said some need instruction and that they don't know *my* body or much less how to work it. No kidding. I asked for another glass of wine, politely declined her invitation again, and changed the subject to something else entirely. I will take my chances.

Gratification in the bedroom is a lot more involved than going at it like a couple of monkeys at the zoo and yet is less involved than, say, a scholarly, pantless, conversation about the mons pubis, et al.

Some conversation in the bedroom can be okay, like pillow talk in the aftermath or simple phrases such as "Yes! Right there!" while actively engaged, but outside of that, too many words can be a distraction. For instance, intimacy is not the time to take a satisfaction survey. Asking how he did, how I did, or if "it" was "good" will all lead to poorly rated surveys.

Cartographical questions such as, "Are you there yet?" or "Are you close?" give credence to men's inability to follow directions and the answer is the automatic lie that slips off the tongue as if it were now a part of our genetic makeup, "Yep. About five more minutes."

I've heard the hem and haw of "Did you?" We all know the answer: *If you have to ask, the answer is no.* The other answer will either be a lie, or it will be crude.

Being satisfied isn't always about reaching a climax, though, it certainly can help matters along. It is about being attended to without pressure. It is about paying attention without a time frame. It's about feeling full.

Cheesecake can teach us a lot in that department. It attends to parts of you that you weren't aware needed tending to. No one has to ask if you are done yet. No one has to ask if you enjoyed your cheesecake. Cheesecake renders a hum and an uhm-hmmm of satisfaction. Sometimes my eyes roll back in my head as I close my eyes and sometimes my toes curl. That's what I'm talking about. That is satisfaction.

ONE HAPPY COCONUT

(Coconut Cheesecake with Rhubarb and Strawberry Topping)

INGREDIENTS

Crust

- 1½ cups of graham crackers
- 1½ cups toasted coconut
- 1 T of lemon juice
- ¼ cup sugar
- ½ cup melted butter

Cheesecake

- 4 (8 oz) packages of cream cheese
- 4 large eggs
- ¾ cup of sugar
- 1 (15 oz) can of coconut cream
- ½ cup sour cream
- 1 tsp vanilla extract
- Juice from ½ lemon

Topping

- 1 lb rhubarb, cut into pieces
- 1 T lemon juice
- ½ cup of strawberry jelly
- 2¼ tsp of gelatin

DIRECTIONS:

Preheat oven to 325° F. Grease bottom and sides of a 9" springform pan. Put all dry crust ingredients into a food processor and pulse until fine crumbs. Transfer to a bowl and add butter and lemon juice, mixing until the ingredients stick together. Press the mixture into the bottom and sides of the springform pan. Wrap the pan in a double layer of aluminum foil. Set aside.

In a large bowl, beat cream cheese and sugar until creamy. Add coconut cream, sour cream, vanilla, and lemon. Lastly, beat in the eggs, one at a time, only until blended. Pour cheesecake into springform pan.

Place the springform pan in a large baking pan with about 1" of water to prepare for the water bath. Place in 325° oven and bake for 75–90 minutes. Cheesecake will be stable along the edges and slightly jiggly in the middle. Turn off the oven and allow cheesecake to slowly cool in warm oven for 30 minutes. Remove from oven and cool to room temperature (2 hours). Run a knife along the edge of the springform pan to release cheesecake from pan.

For topping, in a small bowl sprinkle gelatin over ¼ cup of water and let sit for 10 minutes.

In a saucepan, combine jelly and 1 cup of water. Bring to a boil. Add gelatin. Stir. Add rhubarb, reduce heat and simmer until rhubarb is light pink and slightly softened (2–4 minutes). Add lemon juice. Place topping over cheesecake.

Refrigerate for at least 6 hours or overnight. Remove from pan and serve.

24.

THERE IS NO SECRET BEHIND
A GOOD CHEESECAKE

The bottom line is this: I hate secrets. Surprises reserve a time slot for a joyous reveal whereas secrets clash with your upright agenda like a toe stub on a sharp-cornered coffee table.

I'm not talking about Victoria's Secret. There is nothing discreet or covert about what's being sold there. And I'm not talking about secrets in the culinary world. They dangle secrets like charms on a cheap bracelet: secret sauce, secret recipe, secret ingredient, and so on. They are hush-hush about things that aren't really all that classified. I mean, everyone knows it's either nutmeg, a pinch of sugar, or a teaspoon of bourbon. No surprise. No secret. We just play along to be nice. No big deal.

All things undisclosed should be so obvious or apparent. It would make secrets much easier to accept. They also shouldn't expose themselves at 3 a.m. or while driving cross-country, belted, and confined next to someone who's going to lose their sh*t once the secret's out. There's no good time to uncover the abstruse, but maybe afternoons are slightly better than the wee hours of the night. Maybe open fields are better than a cab of a moving truck

From earrings that weren't mine that were left on the bedstand, feminine products that weren't mine in a waste bin, to photos I didn't want to see, and porn collections I didn't want to find, secrets became my Whac-A-Mole as they popped up almost everywhere.

With a few too many for good measure, my view of relationships, and my trust therein, skewed. Worse, my trust in myself, my ability to discern secrets from truth, has gone awry.

My intuition, with the couth of a tattletale, always says I told you so. She calls me gullible. She hasn't been wrong. She's just been ignored.

The other part of my brain has created a set of rules and a list of questions to ask in the ongoing parley of dating. I ask questions like, "How long have you been divorced?" and "What types of things does your ex say about you?" and "Are we in a monogamous relationship?"

These feel fair to ask and I am simple enough to believe that the answers are all true. Because why would anyone lie?

It was no surprise when I met the cyclist that the days and weeks that followed were an interrogation on intentions.

I had made the decision to bike across Iowa. It was an organized ride of twenty thousand cyclists of whom I had no motive of making friends, hooking up, or falling in love. I was there to enjoy spending all day on my bicycle with my only agenda being to eat ice cream and pie made by local farmers who sold it along the cycling route.

It was a six-day trek across the state and as day two ended, the unexpected happened. A looming shadow fell over me. As I texted my friends who were cycling with me on this journey, a hand slowly approached my shoulder.

In front of me stood a former defensive tackle, 6' 3", blocking both the sun and the air, reaching for my shoulder with something in his hand. Stopped by my death stare that threatened to take his big ass down if he continued with whatever he was going to do, I resumed contacting my friends. He recommended trying to get my attention.

Annoyed, my response to his antics should have reduced his pursuit to dust. Yet he persisted. He said hello. He said hello again. He bent down to say hello closer to my line of vision. He introduced himself. He introduced himself again. He said he was trying to give me a sticker from his cycling team, Team Bastard. He again introduced himself including his team's tagline, "I'm a Bastard."

Unable to resist, my face cracked a smile. When I finally looked up, I knew I was a goner. He had a big, white smile, dimples, and eyes that looked remarkably like the world as seen from space. He bought me a beer, met my friends, and we ended up chatting until late in the evening, finalizing the night with plans to meet again for breakfast the following day.

After a high-carb breakfast of biscuits and gravy, we pedaled the traffic-free highway laid before us. My interrogation of him began within the first mile and he didn't hesitate to answer everything I threw at him.

He said he was divorced with three almost-adult kids. He considered himself liberal in a conservative way and didn't consider himself to be religious, though he did go to church occasionally. He never owned a minivan and when he was in college, playing college ball, he was also studying classical music theory to better understand the music he played.

A football player who not only studied classical music, but played it? He was like a living version of the shirtless firemen-holding-kittens calendar!

The dichotomy of his hobbies made the cross-examination interesting as well as laughable. He had piqued my interest, for sure.

The remaining days of the trip were cycled together, meeting up for breakfast and saying goodnight when the evening bonfire died down. Each night, he asked for a good-night kiss and each night I said no, reminding him that I wasn't in Iowa motoring for a man.

I got one anyway.

After Iowa, the communication continued and the next thing you know we were in a long-distance relationship. My brain was so mad at my heart for that. I tried so hard to mentally talk myself out of feelings.

He tried his best to get those feelings to come out. He'd fly me in for dates. He'd send flowers on the weekends that he was away. For months, we'd have sweet little getaways to quiet little towns a half a day's drive away from wherever we were together. Much like when we first met, he softened my steely resolve through persistence. My heart had turned to mush. I was falling in love.

Looking forward to a future that we dreamed about together, I was visionless about the nuanced pieces that didn't fit. I felt often at one arm's length while the other pulled me in. Honestly, I questioned myself, assuming that too many years single had left me unable to fully receive the love that was being offered. The answers were in the details.

In Iowa, he was liberal. At home he was only liberal with helpings of food and pontificating on conservative ideals. In Iowa, he declared himself to be spiritual and not religious, yet was a deacon in his parish. He eventually shared with me his belief that because I didn't practice what he practiced, I was pedaling the downward slope to hell. He said he prayed for me. Don't ask me why I let these things slide. I just did.

The truth was, honestly, that I accepted these little lies because I was so tired of being alone, that any relationship felt better than none. Any differences seemed small compared to my desire to be coupled, to have a companion, to think about a future *with* someone. I was willing to overlook a lot.

He flew to my hometown with the specific goal of driving the moving truck to his hometown, moving me across the country so we could be closer. With the furniture on the truck, a key to my new apartment in hand, and a promise that a teenage son was going to help with the heavy lifting, I was feeling lucky to be in love and have a partner for these things.

I asked him to call his son and give him an ETA of our arrival. He didn't. A little while later, I asked again. He didn't call again. With my final request and his final delay, I asked him why he wasn't calling his son. He said, "He's not ready for this. It's too soon for him." Confused, I asked for clarification.

He whimpered out something inaudible.

He repeated it for me, and I was not quite sure I heard him right.

I had him repeat it a third time.

He was still married.

Mother F*cker.

In the ugly mess of the aftermath of truth, he backpedaled. He apologized. He said he thought I knew. He said he was sorry again as he promised a divorce was coming. I couldn't hear him. I was buried beneath the rubble of broken dreams, shattered trust, a flood of tears, and the despair that pounces on the broken heart.

Things slowly started to make sense: the out-of-town trips, hotel stays when I'd visit because he said he had the kids that weekend, the little lies. With each veil lifted, I broke a little more. I kept breaking until there was nothing more left to break. That was a big secret and it rightfully destroyed us. Years later, I am still mired in the shame of my naivete. Climbing over the wall of compromise that I built out of expectation, loneliness, and desire, drained aspirations of ever being in a relationship again.

I had asked the questions and I received the answers I wanted to hear but also lost the important, truth-abiding minutia to the blinders of possibility.

Once upon a time, I would have fought for the promises given. I would have tried to wait this thing out. I would have held on to the idea of love even though the lies were clear evidence that it wasn't there.

Not this time. This time I just sank to the lowest point of where I was and sat there for a while, piecing myself back together, slowly but surely. I called my girlfriends. I lit some candles, took some long baths, went for even longer walks. I made art, made new friends, and found my community. I was learning.

When the bottom falls out, there's a new bottom. From there, the climb begins again. It wasn't what I wanted or hoped, but it was what it was. As I milled around in the darkness of my despair, in a city that was foreign to me, there were some truths that came to me about my own patterns, projections, predictions, and presumptions. This time, I had to ask *myself* the questions knowing that the answers would take me to deeper bottoms, louder truths, and most likely closer to more meaning and bigger faith than I could conceive in the moments of feeling broken. I had to shift my trust to an open-ended, unanswerable catechism of my personal truth. Healing is a different kind of pain: an honest one.

The truth is that I had to learn to accept my circumstances and love myself for my ability to navigate through them. The truth is that I am never really alone because I have family, friends, and faith with me all the time. The truth is that I could no longer choose to not see what I didn't want to see. The hurt had cracked open the parts of me that I had hidden from myself.

Cheesecake doesn't have secrets. There is nothing to own but cheesecake. Cheesecake isn't secretly married. It isn't hiding a secret double life. Cheesecake has integrity. Everything you want to know about a cheesecake is all laid out for you in plain text. Cheesecake hides nothing and has no surprises to spring on you that will break your heart. The truth is, there is no secret behind a good cheesecake.

NO SECRET TO THIS CHEESECAKE
(Bitter Orange and Dark Chocolate Cheesecake)

INGREDIENTS:

Crust
- 1 cup graham cracker crumbs
- 1 cup gingersnap crumbs
- 1 cup almonds
- ⅓ cup brown sugar
- 1 stick (8 T) butter, melted
- Pinch of salt

Cheesecake
- 3 (8 oz packages) cream cheese, room temperature
- 1 cup sour cream
- 1 cup granulated sugar
- 3 eggs plus 1 yolk, room temperature
- 2 tsp vanilla extract
- ¼ tsp almond extract
- ¼ cup orange marmalade
- ¼ cup fresh orange juice
- Zest from 1 orange
- 2 T dark chocolate, cut into the smallest pieces possible

Topping
- ½ cup orange marmalade
- 2 T orange juice
- 1 tsp vanilla extract
- Fresh raspberries

DIRECTIONS:

Preheat oven to 350° F. Grease bottom and sides of a 9" springform pan. In a food processor, place nuts and graham crackers, pulsing until they are crumbs. Add sugar and mix. Add butter and combine until the mixture holds together. Press the mixture into the bottom and sides of the springform pan. Bake for 8 minutes. Set aside to cool. Wrap the pan in a double layer of aluminum foil, and place it in a large baking pan to prepare for the water bath. Set aside.

In a small bowl, combine the orange juice, orange zest, orange marmalade, vanilla, and almond extracts. Set aside.

In a large bowl, beat the cream cheese until smooth. Add sugar and sour cream. Mix until smooth. Add eggs and yolk, incorporating one egg at a time and mixing until smooth. Add the orange mixture and mix slowly until combined. Stir in the secret ingredient: chocolate bits. Pour batter into the prepared pan. Fill baking pan with 1" hot water to prepare for the water bath. Bake cheesecake at 350° for 60–75 minutes. Sides should be set, and center will be a little jiggly.

When cheesecake has baked for 60 minutes, let cheesecake rest in a warm oven for 30 minutes. Remove from oven and cool to room temperature. Run a knife along the inside edge of the pan to release the cheesecake and prevent cracking.

In a small saucepan, melt marmalade with orange juice. Add vanilla. Stir. Pour over cheesecake. Top with raspberries. Refrigerate at least 6 hours or until ready to serve.

25.

CHEESECAKE IS ALWAYS THERE WHEN YOU NEED IT

With so much time as a single person—single mom, single income, single voice amongst the choir, I have attended a lot of things solo: Christmas parties, family gatherings, work events, funerals, weddings, and so on. At family gatherings, relatives wonder if I'm okay. At weddings, I'm that one adult on the dance floor with the little kids. At funerals, I'm the one being openly prayed for by old people. I've often heard mumblings to Saint Jude, patron saint of hopeless causes, as I walked to the front of the service to pay my respects. I've actually been given a St. Jude pocket coin. I've since lost it.

I've had my fortune told, my tarot read, and burned some sage, all with the good intention of not attending any more events as a party of one. I am often a victim of my own optimism.

Dates can be hard to come by, especially if there is a dress requirement or the expectation of dancing involved. The worst part about going to any event alone is that I don't have someone to appreciate the tremendous amount of effort I put into looking nice for the occasion. There is no one to say, "You look beautiful."

Another downside is that friends and family often serve as stand-ins, reiterating through their pity-filled acceptance, my challenges with finding a taker for the second ticket to just about anything.

On one such affair, long after I had settled in to having an unused ticket, my brother called me from the West Coast where he lives and said, "Cinderella, put on your glass slippers. You have a date for the ball."

He flew across the country, tuxedo in tow, and filled the chair next to me in a way that only a big brother can. I cannot thank him enough for being such a great brother and for showing me where the bar is supposed to be set. He even threw in a compliment for good measure. Pity never felt so good.

That bar that my brother set came crashing down a short time later, breaking not only the chair next to me, but the table, the centerpiece, and my heart.

Long before that crash-and-smash summer, I took a leap of faith and ventured into a new career. This leap left some folks in my life pouring sarcasm like Morton's salt on the fire of my passions, wishing me well in my job search. Their support left me wondering about whose basement I would live in when every last fiber of my faith had been shredded by the tug-of-war between what I believed possible and what they believed wasn't.

I worked my ass off to make my career everything I believed that it could be. As a single person with few prospects, this was easy to do.

In just a few short years, I was working full time in a program that I designed and created. I became president of the local chapter of the association and an adjunct professor at a university. With the career beginning to flourish, life, in general, felt more on track. I started dating again.

I had found someone who seemed to be reaching for my otherwise impossible bar and who was willing to take the extra ticket. We both worked in the helping professions and found importance in giving back. We met while volunteering. This, according to the rule books, is how you are supposed to meet someone: by doing something that you love. Check.

Then, according to the rule books, you are supposed to do things together that you both enjoy. Check. Values. Beliefs. Goals. Check. Check and check.

He had some quirks that I could handle. He danced like an ape in mating season. He loved the color brown. He put his food to his nose before putting it in his mouth. Odd but okay.

Solidly over the one-year mark, I leaned in.

As I rested comfortably in the relationship, my career went to the next level, winning an international award in a world-renowned agency. I was high for a month on the news and busy making arrangements for the award ceremony in Chicago.

It was to be an evening of celebrating beyond measure.

The night before the biggest event of my career, my leaning in left me falling flat on the floor. My boyfriend called to say that he wasn't coming to Chicago. Like vinegar in a milkshake, the conversation got real sour real fast. He insisted that he couldn't fit this event into his schedule. He insisted that something came up. He had to cut the grass. He said he just couldn't make it.

The devastation of this blow rendered me speechless. It felt like it came out of nowhere. Gone was the idea that we were a couple. Gone was the companionship that was supposed to be supportive and carry me through any situation, including good ones. Gone was the hand to hold. Gone was the filled chair. Gone was the idea, once again, of a happy ending.

After much ado, I offered him until departure time to change his mind, pleading that whatever it was that made him not want to come, we could get through it. The train left at 4 p.m.

On the platform, with my hair professionally done, full makeup, and in my evening gown, I waited. I waited. I waited some more. I had faith in this man's ability to make the right decision … right up until the train left the station. As I boarded, I heard it. I heard it through the gasping for air: my heart shattered into a million little pieces. Alone, I found a seat near a window, placed my perfectly coiffed head against it and cried all the way to Chicago, feeling alone on a train full of people.

These waterworks weren't romantic little tears that gently dropped from my eyes to the lap of my beautiful dress. No. This was an ugly cry: hands over the face, unrelenting stream of snot, and loud, uncontrollable wails.

By the end of the train ride, the well of tears had run dry and my face had been washed clean in the process. The happiest moment of my career was overshadowed with a painful sadness and a wave of loneliness unlike I had felt before.

At the station, a limousine awaited. The driver opened the door for me, and I slid into the empty back seat, making my way across the vast emptiness to the farthest corner I could find. With my head against a new window, new tears came down, this time alone with no one around. The car dropped me onto a red carpet in front of the hotel. I looked like something found on the floor after the after-party.

The sliding glass doors opened and what I saw next brought me to my knees.

Seven of my friends were there and they formed a semicircle around the door. When I came through, each and every one of them wrapped themselves around me in a big hug and literally carried me up to a suite for fresh makeup, hair fixing, champagne, and mix of condolences and celebrations. They saw that the glass slippers had been shattered by the bar that fell, and they gave me new shoes. They reached for the bar that was still rolling on the floor and placed it back up where it belonged. They promised to use it as a weapon should the need arise.

It was a night to remember, not just for the accolade, but because I knew all the way to my soul that the cure for heartbreak and feeling alone was to surround myself with the bonds of people who are there with me through it all. They were my godsent gifts and the real award of the evening and of a lifetime.

All the years before and all the years after, the unwavering steel support of my girlfriends has carried me, lifted me, cheered with me, grown with and filled me with a deep gratitude. They fed me with love, bubbly, and—yes—cheesecake. THIS was love. True love.

CINDERELLA'S SLIPPER

(Champagne Cheesecake with Champagne and Fig Reduction)

INGREDIENTS:

Crust

- 1½ cups graham cracker crumbs
- 1 cup almonds, toasted and cooled
- ⅔ cup sugar
- ½ cup butter, melted

Cheesecake

- 4 (8 oz) packages cream cheese, room temperature
- 1 cup sugar
- 2 T fig jam
- ½ cup sour cream plus ½ cup for topping
- ½ tsp vanilla extract
- 3 eggs
- ⅔ cup champagne reduction (below)
- 2 T cornstarch

Champagne Reduction

- 3 cups sparkling wine
- Zest of one lemon
- 5 raspberries
- 1 cup fig jam

Topping

- ½ cup fig jam
- ½ cup sour cream
- Water

DIRECTIONS:

To make the champagne reduction, place all ingredients for reduction in a large saucepan and bring to a simmer. As fruit softens, smash it to release the juices. Simmer until reduced by half. Strain into a bowl. Set aside.

Preheat oven to 350° F. Grease bottom and sides of a 9" springform pan. In a food processor, combine graham crackers, almonds, and sugar. Process until they are crumbs. Add butter and combine until the mixture holds together. Press the mixture into the bottom and sides of the springform pan. Bake for 8 minutes. Set aside to cool.

Once cool, wrap the pan in a double layer of aluminum foil, and place in a large baking pan to prepare for the water bath.

In a large bowl, beat the cream cheese until smooth. Add sugar and sour cream. Beat until smooth. Add fig jam and mix. Add champagne reduction and cornstarch. Beat. Add eggs, one at a time and beat until combined. Add vanilla. Mix until blended.

Pour batter into the prepared pan. Add hot water to the baking pan and bake cheesecake for 50–60 minutes. Mix ½ cup champagne reduction with ½ cup sour cream. Pour over cheesecake and bake for 10 minutes more or until edges are firm and center is jiggly. Turn off oven and let cheesecake cool in oven for half an hour. Remove from oven and cool to room temperature (about 2 hours). Run a knife along the inside edge of the pan to release the cheesecake and prevent cracking.

In a small saucepan, whisk together jam and sour cream, over low heat. If mixture thickens, add 1 tablespoon of water. (Mixture should be the consistency of gravy.) Pour over cheesecake.

Place cheesecake in refrigerator and cool at least 6 hours or until serving.

Serve with fresh raspberries and figs and drizzle with champagne reduction.

26.

SAMPLE PLATTER

A little bit of this. A little bit of that. Plain vanilla. Chocolate. Some with big nuts. Some with none. Some with a cherry. Others with a shot of bourbon. The sample platter lets us try a bit of everything and decide what we'd like to have more of and what we never want to have again.

I've got a list going of what I'd like more of and a book about what I never want to have again.

The sample platter of single life is called dating.

We all want different things and yet, we all want the same things. Some things seem to depend on mood. Others on the weather. Some things are in the details and others are in the broader picture. Love resides in all.

The details that matter will differ from person to person. For me, I enjoy the small, sweet nothings like a sticky note left in the book I'm reading that says, "I love you like the words love this page." I love the feeling of a hand in the small of my back and hate the feeling of a hand on my ass. It's an important detail to know the difference between the two. I love a man who loves to cook. When he knows how to spice things up, *he knows how to spice things up.* He knows how to pay attention to nuance. These are the details that paint the broader picture.

Unfortunately, the samples I chose may have had a smattering of details that seemed appealing, but the larger platter came up empty in meeting the whole of what I was looking for.

With a cheesecake sample platter, you don't need to see the whole of what slice is now before you. You can love the slice from beginning to end. You can also be indecisive. You can vacillate between slices, bouncing back and forth to decide which one hits the spot the best and no one is going to label you a floozy. You can go back to the same cheesecake slice again and again and no one will chide you about needing to let that one go. You can have friends over, and everyone can sample the samples, and no one is going to call the police or the pastor. There is nothing that no one doesn't want on a cheesecake sample platter.

THE SAMPLE PLATTER

INGREDIENTS:

Crust

- 1 cup almonds
- 2 sleeves of graham crackers
- ⅓ cup sugar
- ½ cup butter, melted
- 1 T lemon juice

Cheesecake base

- 4 (8 oz) packages cream cheese, room temperature
- 1 cup sour cream, room temperature
- ½ cup sugar
- ½ cup honey
- ½ tsp vanilla
- 3 eggs plus 2 egg yolks
- 1 T cornstarch

(SEE CHART FOR FLAVORING)

DIRECTIONS:

Preheat oven to 350° F. Grease sides and bottoms of three (6") springform pans.

For crust, place nuts and graham crackers into a food processor and pulse until they are crumbs. Add sugar and flour and pulse until combined. Transfer to a bowl. Add butter and lemon juice. Combine until the mixture holds together.

Divide the mixture between the three pans (about 2 cups each). Press the mixture into the bottom and sides of each springform pan. Bake at 350° for 10 minutes. Set aside to cool. Wrap the pans in a double layer of aluminum foil, and place into a separate baking pan for each to prepare for the water bath.

In a bowl, beat cream cheese until smooth. Add sour cream, sugar, and honey, one at a time and mix until blended. Scrape sides of bowl often to ensure even mixing. Add vanilla and mix. Add eggs, one at a time, and mix until blended. Add in cornstarch. Mix until well combined and creamy.

Divide cheesecake base into 3 bowls (about 2 cups each). Add flavoring of your choice to each bowl (see chart for flavoring quantities and toppings). Mix until flavors are well combined. Pour over prepared crusts.

Add 1" of hot water to each pan and carefully place pans with water and cheesecakes into the oven. Bake at 350° for 45 minutes or until sides are set and the centers jiggle. Turn off oven and let cheesecakes rest for half an hour.

Remove cheesecakes from the oven and cool to room temperature (about 2 hours). Run a knife along the inside edge of the pan to release the cheesecakes and prevent cracking.

Prepare toppings for each cheesecake (refer to chart). Refrigerate at least 6 hours or until ready to serve.

Coffee and Cardamom	Lemon and Thyme	Saffron and Orange Blossom
¼ tsp cardamom 2 T strong brewed coffee Topping: 1 tsp brewed coffee 2 T butter 2 T brown sugar 1 tsp corn syrup *Heat over medium heat until boiling. Boil 2 minutes. Pour over cheesecake.*	1 T lemon zest 1 T lemon juice 2 T lemon syrup* Topping: 2 T lemon curd 1 tsp lemon syrup* *Warm mixture. Whisk until blended. Pour over cheesecake.*	1 T orange zest 1 T orange marmalade 1 tsp orange-blossom water Pinch of saffron and turmeric Topping: 1 T orange marmalade 1 tsp orange-blossom water 1 T sour cream *Warm mixture. Whisk until blended. Pour over cheesecake.*

Strawberry and Balsamic	Plum and Cracked Pepper	Orange and Dark Chocolate
2 tsp strawberry jam 2 tsp balsamic reduction* Sliced strawberries, (marinated in reduction and placed in a layer with batter) Topping: *Place fresh, sliced strawberries. Drizzle with reduction sauce.*	2 T plum syrup* ½ tsp cornstarch Cracked pepper Topping: 1 T raspberry jam 1 T plum syrup Cracked pepper Small pinch of salt *Whisk jam and sauce together. Pour over cheesecake. Top with salt and pepper.*	1 T orange marmalade 1 T orange zest 1 T orange juice 1½ T dark chocolate, chopped fine Topping: 2 T orange marmalade ½ tsp water Fresh raspberries *Warm marmalade and water, whisking until liquid. Pour over cheesecake. Garnish with fresh raspberries.*

Champagne and Fig	Chocolate Hazelnut	New York Style
⅓ cup champagne reduction* 1 T fig jam Topping: 1 T fig jam 1 tsp champagne reduction* 1 T sour cream *Warm jam and champagne reduction. Whisk until smooth. Add sour cream. Whisk. Pour over cheesecake.*	⅓ cup hazelnut spread 1 T dark chocolate, chopped fine Topping: 2 T dark chocolate, chopped fine 1 T heavy cream *Heat heavy cream until hot. Pour over chocolate. Stir until smooth. Pour over cheesecake.*	1 tsp lemon zest 1 tsp lemon juice Topping: ½ tsp vanilla extract ½ cup sour cream 1 T sugar *Combine topping ingredients and pour over cheesecake with 10 minutes remaining for cheesecake to cook. Bake for 10 minutes.*

SYRUPS AND REDUCTIONS

*LEMON AND THYME SYRUP
- 1 cup water
- ½ cup sugar
- 5 sprigs of fresh thyme
- ½ stalk of fresh lemongrass, smashed
- Juice and zest from ½ lemon

In a saucepan, combine ingredients for syrup and bring to a boil. Reduce heat and simmer for 10 minutes. Strain over a bowl and allow mixture to cool.

*STRAWBERRY AND BALSAMIC REDUCTION
- ½ cup balsamic vinegar
- ½ cup red wine
- 3 T brown sugar
- Zest of one lemon
- 5 raspberries
- 2 large strawberries, diced
- Plus 3 strawberries sliced thin to marinate in reduction

In a large saucepan, combine first six ingredients and bring to a simmer. As fruit softens, smash it to release the juices. Simmer until reduced by half. Strain into a bowl. Add sliced strawberries to marinate. Set aside.

*CHAMPAGNE AND FIG REDUCTION

- 1 cup champagne or brut
- 1 T lemon zest
- 3 raspberries
- ⅓ cup fig jam

In a saucepan, combine ingredients and bring to a simmer. As fruit softens, smash it to release the juices. Simmer until reduced by half. Strain into a bowl. Set aside.

*PLUM SYRUP

- 1 plum, cut into quarters
- ¼ cup raspberries
- ¼ cup red wine
- 1 T sugar
- 1 tsp lemon juice

In a saucepan, combine ingredients and bring to a simmer. As fruit softens, smash it to release the juices. Simmer until reduced by half. Strain into a bowl. Set aside.

27.

THERE IS NO SHORTAGE OF GOOD CHEESECAKE

Labeling a cheesecake "good" is redundant, obvious, and unnecessary. If you tell people that you have a good cheesecake, they may ask if you've ever had a bad one. You will both laugh about that and begin a conversation about other things that don't exist like the jackalope, the Easter Bunny, political neutrality, and unbiased opinions.

If you tell people that you have a good man, they will congratulate you like you won the lottery.

Having been on the dating scene for a while, I can tell you that meeting someone is the first hurdle in the race for a man. Advice comes in that tells you "Do what you love," "Step out of your comfort zone," and "Place yourself where they are."

Been there, done that. I met a lot of other single women.

This leads me to ask, where are the good men are hiding? What happened to them? What rock have I not yet lifted? I've been told that my standards are too high by some and that they aren't high enough by others. I've been told that it's me and I've been told that it's not me. I've been told that the good ones are all taken. Whatever the perspective or whatever the truth, one thing remains perfectly clear: I do not have this issue with cheesecake.

I'm eternally hopeful that cheesecake will meet its match someday in a man who exceeds the qualities I find in cheesecake.

I'm trying.

I've been on a lot of first dates, and I've eaten a lot of cheesecake. Here are some results:

I had a first date with a guy who, upon meeting, proceeded to tell me all about how his ex-wife tried to rake him over the coals financially and how he showed her. "She got nothing," he laughed. Very funny. I'm sure his two young daughters appreciate his humor, too. The most telling bit from this date was the fact that I asked him a non-related question. I asked him what a typical day looks like in his world. He went off on his own little non sequitur tirade. Someone needs to claim his Baggage. No more dates with Mr. Angrily-Stuck-in-Yesterday.

I had a first date in a bookstore with a guy whose profile said he was 6' 1" tall. When he tapped me on the shoulder, I expected to turn around and look up. I turned around and looked him square in the eye. The last time I checked, I was 5' 7". Someone is bad at math. Turned out, he enjoyed fantasy. He was a big fan of comic books, Marvel movies, and just about anything with aliens. Someone never left sixth grade. I see where the math problem lay. No more dates with Junior.

I had a first date with a guy at a small café. Each time I asked him what he did for a living, he'd tell me what his dad did. I asked him again and he said his brother was an asshole. I suspect he was unemployed. I think that he may have lived in his father's basement and that his brother must have been mad about it. No more dates with Mr. Unmotivated.

I had a first date with a guy who spent the entire time telling me how great he was. He was so busy talking about himself that he forgot to see if I even cared. I didn't. He didn't ask a single question of me or even make a gesture in my direction. The future of our relationship flashed before my eyes, and I saw myself knitting sweaters during intercourse and him high-fiving himself at the end. Nope. No more dates for Mr. Self-Absorbed.

It seems to me that dating should not be this disappointing. Dating has been the Euro-Disney in the adventurous theme park I call my life.

Thank goodness there's cheesecake. My first taste of cheesecake and I was hooked.

The relationship has only grown and blossomed since then. Cheesecake has seen me through a lot of heartache and has been the impetus for learning, understanding, and healing. Cheesecake plumps out the thin spots and mends the parts that need mending. It brings people together, and it unites us all in good taste and decadence.

Cheesecake won't make me thinner. But it also won't add salt to the wound of being single in a coupled culture. It may wreck my diet and give me cause to do things like running, but it won't make me want to run away crying. No tears have been shed because of cheesecake. Cheesecake is worth every calorie, every pound, and every busted zipper. I'd love to say the same about men, but thus far, cheesecake is the winner.

Cheesecake is better than men.

WHEN LIFE GIVES YOU LEMONS

(Lemon and Thyme Cheesecake with Lemongrass)

INGREDIENTS:

Crust

- 1 cup almonds
- 1 cup graham crackers
- 1 cup gingersnap cookies
- ½ cup butter, melted

Cheesecake

- 3 (8 oz) packages cream cheese, room temperature
- ½ cup sour cream, room temperature
- ½ cup sugar
- ¼ cup honey
- ½ tsp vanilla extract
- ¼ cup lemongrass and thyme syrup (see below)
- Juice and zest of ½ lemon
- 3 eggs
- 2 T cornstarch
- 1 T lemon curd

Topping

- ¼ cup water
- ¼ cup lemongrass and thyme syrup
- ¼ cup sour cream or yogurt
- ¼ cup lemon curd
- 1 tsp gelatin

Lemongrass and thyme syrup

- 1 cup water
- ½ cup sugar

- 5 sprigs of fresh thyme
- ½ stalk of fresh lemongrass, smashed
- Juice and zest from ½ lemon

DIRECTIONS:

Preheat oven to 350° F. Grease bottom and sides of a 9" springform pan. For crust, place nuts, graham crackers, and cookies into a food processor and pulse until they are crumbs. Transfer to a bowl. Add butter. Combine until the mixture holds together. Press the mixture into the bottom and sides of the springform pan. Bake at 350° for 10 minutes. Set aside to cool. Wrap the pan in a double layer of aluminum foil, and set into a baking pan to prepare for the water bath.

In a saucepan, combine ingredients for syrup and bring to a boil. Reduce heat and simmer for 10 minutes. Strain over a bowl and allow mixture to cool.

In a bowl, beat cream cheese until smooth. Add sour cream, sugar, and honey, one at a time and mix until blended. Add lemongrass and thyme syrup and blend until combined. Add juice and zest of lemon. Blend until combined. Scrape sides of bowl often to ensure even mixing. Add vanilla. Add eggs, one at a time, and mix until blended. Add in cornstarch and lemon curd. Mix until well combined and creamy. Pour over crust. Fill large baking pan with 1" hot water. Bake for 55–65 minutes or until sides are set and the center jiggles. Turn off oven and let cheesecake rest for half an hour.

Remove cheesecake from oven and cool to room temperature (about 2 hours).

In a saucepan, mix water, syrup, lemon curd, and sour cream. Heat until warm and whisk until smooth. Once mixture is warm, sprinkle gelatin over top and whisk until combined. Pour over cheesecake.

Refrigerate at least 6 hours or until ready to serve.

28.

CHEESECAKE IS CONSISTENT

My oldest brother, the one with the well-intended misguidance, offered an observation. He said that when couples get divorced, women, like me, get into therapy, go back to school, pursue dreams, and ultimately improve who we are. He noted that I had been on a course to live a more fulfilled life.

"The men," he said, "do nothing beyond blame women for the divorce." He added that it is the men that other women left who are the ones in the dating pool. He apologized on behalf of his gender.

It was hard to admit that he might be right. We all know how brotherly advice can go.

He was right, however, in how much I was trying to work on myself. I had gone back for a master's degree. I had started a new career. I went to therapy. I attended boot camp at 5:30 a.m. and yoga at night. I bought a subscription to *Healthy Living* and by God, I was going to live healthy.

I took my daughter to Hawaii so we could take surfing lessons. We went to Colorado so we could learn how to downhill ski. I learned to waterski. I bought a road bike and biked across Iowa. Twice.

My confidence in my own sustainability grew. A weighted blanket and a heating pad replaced any need to be held close while I slept. The laughter of good friends replaced the tears of not-so-good relationships and all the while, cheesecakes appeared in my kitchen.

Baking was my coping tool. The metaphors found helped me to sort through and identify relationship things that worked well and things that didn't. I learned that when things go too fast (like setting the mixer on high while incorporating eggs which adds too much air to the batter)—it will later lead to deep cracks. Eventually, the cheesecake will fall apart. Some relationships had gone too fast and fell apart.

I learned that if ingredients ran too cold or were heated too quickly, it led to inconsistency in the batter such as a lumpy or unevenly flavored cheesecake. Consistency happens when the ingredients come to room temperature slowly over time. This doesn't mean that things don't heat up later. It just means that extremes aren't beneficial when looking for stabilization.

Be aware of temperature and beware the guy that runs hot and cold. It almost goes without saying and, unfortunately, most of us have probably experienced that guy. He can't decide if he's coming or going. He likes you until he doesn't. He will do things like suggest going to a movie and then complain that all you ever want to do is watch movies. He will tell you things that he later denies, leaving you guessing if what you heard was what you heard.

Inconsistency is when he says he knew he wanted to date you because he admired your independence, and yet wouldn't leave your side for a second because "that's what couples do." Inconsistency is when he boasts that he loves your adventurous spirit and go-get-'em attitude but later tells you that you're always running around, and that he prefers date night in front of the television with a pizza. Inconsistency is telling a woman that she's smart and then talking to her like she's stupid. It's called dating a narcissist. It's called gaslighting and it is unkind. I've been on too many dates with guys like this. They love bomb with too many gifts that are too big for the occasion, with too many texts and calls in a day. It is too much attention, and it pulls you away from your own life to make you isolated and alone in his.

It's confusing because limerence is delightful and feels a lot like effervescence all over and the inconsistent guy feels like seltzer and then feels like slamming seltzer. Still bubbles but a different kind.

I have set my sights higher; time to focus on me.

Last month, I took a workshop on how to live a better life through following your dreams. I've dreamed big and in technicolor. These aspirations were, in my mind's eye, based on the belief that love will change everything; it will solve every puzzle, answer every question, and solidify my idea of success. The love that will change everything, the one we are really dying to experience, is the love of self.

I asked myself, "If I don't love me, who will?"

So, I began taking myself on dates. I went dancing. I went to dinner. I went to art exhibitions, plays, took long walks, and lit candles just for me. I buy myself flowers because how I treat myself is how others will treat me back. I am leading by example.

I aspired to greater things in hopes of meeting the man who can take my lead, step in, and keep up.

Meditation groups improved my focus. Hot yoga shaped up my stamina.

I decided that I would not wither away waiting for another's love, rather revitalize myself in its pursuit. Though healthier and more attentive, the fantasy of infatuation has thus far fallen flat.

Meeting my beloved is still high on the roster of things I'd like to accomplish. It's still on the bucket list: fall in love, stay in love. As the temperature of my life remains steady at a comfortable yes-degree, I'm hopeful that the even keel of Mr. Right exists and his consistency makes for a smooth, sweet experience beyond the kitchen, out of the springform pan and lasts long after the plate cleared of its contents.

As for the quest to find that perfect cheesecake, it's always the one I've just made and am now ready to slice and share.

THE VACILLATOR

(Cracked Pepper and Plum Non-Bake Cheesecake)

INGREDIENTS:

Crust
- 2 cups graham cracker crumbs
- 1 cup pecans
- ⅓ cup brown sugar
- ½ cup butter, melted
- Pinch of salt

Cheesecake
- 2 (8 oz) packages cream cheese
- ½ cup powdered sugar
- ½ cup plum sauce plus ½ cup for gelatin mix
- ½ cup sugar
- 1 package gelatin
- 3 T cornstarch
- 1 cup whipping cream, whipped to stiff peaks
- 1 tsp vanilla extract
- Pinch of salt
- Cracked pepper

Plum sauce
- 2 large, ripe plums
- ½ cup raspberries
- ½ cup water
- ½ cup red wine
- ¼ cup sugar
- 1 T lemon juice

Topping
- ½ cup raspberry jam
- ¼ cup water
- 1 T cornstarch
- Salt and cracked pepper

DIRECTIONS:

For the crust, place the graham crackers and nuts in a food processor and pulse until they are crumbs. Transfer to a bowl. Add sugar, salt, and butter. Combine until the mixture holds together. Press the mixture into the bottom and sides of the springform pan. Place in the freezer until ready to use.

To make the plum sauce, cut plums into quarters. Remove pits. Place plums, raspberries, water, and wine into a blender and puree. Transfer to a sauté pan and bring to a simmer. Add sugar and lemon juice. Simmer for about 6 minutes to soften plums and reduce wine. Remove from heat and strain over a bowl. Discard the plum meat and raspberry seeds. Set plum sauce aside until ready to use.

In a small bowl, combine sugar, ½ cup of plum sauce, and boiling water. Stir until sugar dissolves. Sprinkle gelatin packet over water. Stir until dissolved. Set aside.

In a large bowl, beat cream cheese and powdered sugar until smooth. Add ½ cup of plum sauce and beat again. Add gelatin mixture and mix until well blended, scraping down the sides often to ensure even mixing. Add cornstarch. Mix well. Add vanilla, pinch of salt, and about ¼ teaspoon of cracked pepper. Mix well. Fold in whipped cream. Pour into the prepared pan. Refrigerate for at least 4 hours.

In a small saucepan, heat raspberry jam, water, and cornstarch over low heat. Whisk until well blended, smooth, and liquid. Remove from heat. Pour over prepared cheesecake. Chill for 30 minutes.

Sprinkle with a pinch of salt. Using a pepper grinder, sprinkle top of cheesecake with cracked pepper. Refrigerate until ready to serve.

EPILOGUE

In a recent conversation about dating, my friends challenged me to define it. Honestly, without the help of a dictionary, the definition was as evasive now as it was in middle school. With the dictionary, it was just a marker in time.

In the note-passing days of my name plus your name equals true love, multiplying hormones overloaded my capacity to delineate our Rubik's-cube vocabulary around who I liked, how much, or what it meant. I could draw hearts and arrows that looked like puffy pillows and shade them in all varieties of pink and red, but I could not tell you the difference between like and *like*-like, or going with someone, or going *out* with someone, or just going together. Our love labels back then were like popped kernels of corn: same flavor but not one like the other. They were all distinctly different.

High school just added mustard to the mystery as we teased out: friends from pals, guy friends from boyfriends, and *hanging* out with from *going* out with. It was a challenge to decipher what was cool, who was cool, and why was cool even a thing because it disappeared the second the last bell rang senior year.

Nowadays it seems that if you didn't start dating and mating in college, you are swiping and winking as a full-on adult. Is online dating *dating* or is it shopping for a date? Does dating start on the first date and if not, when does it officially start? Do you have to like someone or *like*-like them?

One simple question and I was dumbstruck. Crickets chirped where my thoughts used to be. It's not like I haven't done the research. By default, I am an expert on the subject … or a complete abomination. I guess that depends on whether or not you like the book.

Dating is this:
- *It is a willingness to be vulnerable with another human being while also having good boundaries.*
- *It is stepping outside of your comfort zone while also being 100 percent yourself.*
- *It is trying to align with another person while keeping the course of what is important in your life.*
- *It is finding common ground in values, life goals, intimacy, and play.*
- *It is the butterflies of uncertainty while also truly recognizing that this is your person.*
- *It is exploring this new relationship while feeling that this person has somehow always been a part of your life.*

That's what I wanted to say but what spilled out of my piehole was "Good one. Ha-ha."

No one in the group of single adults who had dated or are dating or want to date had a better answer.

"Okay, then, Marianne. What do you want in a relationship?" someone burped out.

"Huh?"

"Do you want a fling, a friend, a friend with benefits, or a long-term relationship?"

The simple answer was the latter, but the phrase *long-term relationship* invoked the same panic I felt when my college boyfriend wanted to talk about my inevitable graduation thirty-five years ago. Fear had gripped my brain like a rabid raccoon in a McDonald's dumpster at 3 a.m. I let the brain bedlam run its course as I thought about what it is that I actually want, which I believe is what we all really want: to love and be loved.

Each and every dating story, along with all the cheesecakes made as a result, were lessons in love. My heart has been broken (and I am certain that I have broken a few in return), but the heart heals, and we try again, always hopeful that this one is *the* one.

Here's the swift kick in the pants about love and *the one*; we are ALL the one.

We are the one we are looking for. There it is. My final answer.

Only when we learn to embrace the imperfect nature of who we are can we let go of the expectations and shaming thoughts of who we think we are supposed to be. Embracing our imperfections allows other people to do the same. We are mirrors, and in looking at ourselves in loving reflection, we realize the potential of what love can hold for each of us. Love is unfinished when we only look outward or when we expect someone to love us greater than we love ourselves. Others cannot fill the void that only we know is there.

The beautiful irony of loving yourself first so that you can meet your match, is that you stop looking. You find that life is full: full of love, friendships, adventures, and cheesecakes.

I'm still hopeful that someday I will have that *last* first date; that this someone will understand that cheesecake is not a stalwart adversary to be knocked off the plate and stomped down, but an ally to understanding how sweet life can be, especially when it is shared.

ACKNOWLEDGEMENTS

Without the pan, cheesecake is just batter in a bowl. Whether it is a springform pan or some other, it is the pan that provides the structure so that everything can set up just right in the prep and then the presentation. The following people have been that for me and more.

For years, I used the idea of this book as a threat to every date that went wrong, and I made empty promises to just about everyone that someday when I had enough time I'd write it all down and wouldn't that be funny. Then along came Avery Caswell, author, publisher, writing coach, cheerleader, and megaphone of encouragement to set my ass down with a pen and a notepad. Through friendship, baked goods, coffee, wine, dinners, and all sorts of other wooing, she cajoled my weaponized idea onto the paper. She held my hand through every stage of the process while I kicked and screamed like a toddler being dropped off on day three to a daycare I no longer liked. I didn't want to do it. I wasn't ready. I wasn't a writer. I wanted to just live in the fantasyland of later. I still feel that way but here we are. My name is on the cover, and you are reading the thing that I actually wrote. Well done, Avery! I couldn't have done it without you!

Much love also goes out to my collective deceased grandmothers, Dorothy and Mary Ann. They were badass women from a different generation who wore the requisite hose in heels, also with slippers, and even in summer. They wore statement jewelry even though their loudest statements in marital wonderland resembled pepper in a casserole.

They had stories they never told that somehow became legendary in our family. And they hated each other. Despite the disdain, I combined them like the oil and vinegar that they were to dress this story salad that was deeply influenced by their wisdom, humor, recipes, and for the characters that they were. I miss them often.

My mom is also a character of formidable strength, humor, and who has an incredible collection of self-made art and opinions that live out loud. I'd be remiss if I didn't give a shout-out to my mom for being one of the strongest women I know. Not in a deadlifting six hundred pounds kind of way, but in the way she championed walking away from unhealthy relationships while peer pressure was on the rest of the gender to practice their best June Cleaver. Her going against the grain allowed us free-rein kids to grow up with our own opinions and our own identities and to define success on our own terms. I'm still trying to define mine, but I know that if I make it to the bestseller list, it's because my mom bought all the copies and is handing them out to all her friends, neighbors, doctors, pharmacist, bank tellers, UPS delivery persons, pool managers, grocery-store checkout clerks, and the people behind her in line. She will hand deliver them to hospital rooms and food lines if she must. She's that kind of mom.

My brothers, who make varying appearances in the book, have been my lifelong bodyguards, mechanics, and teachers. I could not have chosen more loving, caring, or dedicated punches to the shoulder than Dave and Aaron. Sure, our teenage years tested our tether and pushed our mom to the bottom of every brandy Manhattan in her hand, but whose teenage years didn't, really? We were gloriously angst-y, wild, brilliant, and unaware, just like everyone else. I love my brothers with all my heart, and I don't tell them that. Ever. I probably should.

My firstborn and favorite child who identifies as "an only child, Mom!" is who I do all this for. The positive impact she has had on my life came moments after my then-husband had me take a pregnancy test because he couldn't believe that I was still claiming to have eaten "bad chicken" for the second month in a row. She's my heartbeat, my inspiration, my cheerleader, my teacher, and my soul sister. Her belief in me has taught me to believe in myself as she would say things like, "I know you know the way, Mom. This is just such a great adventure." Yup. She always thought I knew where I was going when I didn't, and she never once feared that we'd run out of money, food, energy, rations, supplies, water, air, ideas, or a way out, even though many times we did. She believes in the success of this book even more than my mom, and together we are counting on sales enough to buy her that brownstone in Brooklyn, a couple of collies, and a few plants. I'm on it, baby girl. I'm on it.

Shout out to the beta readers Terri Strodthoff, Kristin Bradberry, Barbara Singer, Karen Reid, Nancy Murray, and Larry Zuckerman, who provided me with feedback I didn't always want to hear and no donuts to ease the pain. You were supposed to tell me how great the manuscript was, and that I was brilliant and beautiful. I guess that's what my mom is for—so good job on keeping it all so honest. This book would resemble my diary if it weren't for you, so thank you for not letting me put the sex tapes and what happened in Vegas out there for everyone to see. I appreciate your boundaries, your help, your wisdom, and your feedback. Thank you.

Thank you to Nancy Murray for not only beta reading, but providing me with some stellar edits, and to Sasha Boyce who went through this manuscript with a fine-toothed comb with even more edits. This was followed by Debra Nichols who spent endless hours correcting what turned out to be thousands of mistakes and while also never suggesting I take a class on grammar or punctuation. She might be a saint.

Thank you to Danna Mathias Steele for designing the interior of the book and to Jay Cohen for creating the cover.

To Terri, Karen, Vanessa, Bill, Rick, Althea, Jackie, Bridgette, Jay, Lori, Remy, Leslie, Carmella, all the Michaels, Wendy, Lyn, Leeda, Barbara, Natalie/Chris, Jack, and all the other friends whose names I forgot along with your birthdays—Thank you. You are and will always be home to me and I am eternally grateful for your patience as I declined invites to all the fun things so I could sit around my house thinking about writing and wondering what the hell I'm going to tell you all when I never get it done. A lot of time "writing" was actually spent scrolling through TikTok or napping or convincing myself that going to get ice cream would help clear my mind even though I knew it wouldn't. Thanks for understanding and still wanting to be my friend. I'm working on the next book so, well, um … there's that. Please still invite me to things because one of these days I'll put my social anxiety in the laundry room, put my fringe-y pants and dancing shoes on, and come out with full-on jazz hands even if we are only going to the farmers market for eggs.

Finally, let me not forget to thank the men I've dated, known, not known, loved, thought I loved, ran away from, tried to change, and slapped down like a bug in my periphery. I loved you all in my own way and wouldn't have been able to write this book without you. Sure, I always wanted "happily ever after" and a pony, but I think I wanted to write this book more, in an oddly fearful-of-meaningful-relationships sort of way. You have all been my teachers, sometimes to lessons I didn't know I needed to learn, nor did I want to learn, and sometimes to what was possible. If you recognize yourself in any of these stories and didn't like what you read, then you have some choices ahead such as ignore it and it will go away, criticize me, write a bad review, or change. If you didn't recognize yourself in at least part of a story (as many are blended because so many experiences seemed to be on repeat), then read the book again or join a book club that explores the questions at the end of this book. There is a chance that you are not in here, too. It's possible. There will be a second edition, I'm almost certain. Better luck next time then. All that to say, I love you. I really do. This book is not about hating men. It's always been about loving cheesecake a little bit more.

FOOD FOR THOUGHT

(Questions for Your Book Club)

Thank you for reading *Cheesecake Loves My Thighs*. The following questions serve as a guide for discussion—not that you need it given the topic—and some are intended to facilitate awareness and healing.

1. With so many recipes, bake or non-bake, and with many interesting or hard-to-find ingredients, what cheesecake did you bring to the discussion?

2. What chapter stood out to you as both a favorite and a least favorite? How do these two chapters relate to your personal experiences and what flavor of cheesecake might they be?

3. What are some other reasons why cheesecake is better than men?

4. What are some other foods that might work for this metaphor?

5. Fault is rarely a one-sided thing. In several chapters, the author explores her contributions to the issues, such as not setting boundaries, her own insecurities, and her own need to be right. How have you contributed to your relationships, and wouldn't a slice of cheesecake make this dialogue a little sweeter?

6. The first half of the book explores factors of codependency such as neediness, a fear of being alone, needing validation from others, giving too much of oneself, and the like. The second part of the book explore ways to reconcile those issues. How did the author work toward healing?

7. What do you do to help yourself heal from heartbreak and would cheesecake help?

ABOUT THE AUTHOR

Marianne Sprangers author of *Cheesecake Loves My Thighs and 27 Other Reasons Why Cheesecake Is Better Than Men*, blogposts *Cheesecake Is Better Than Men* (www.cheesecakeisbetterthanmen.com) and *Unforeseeably Single* (www.unforeseeablysingle.wordpress.com).

Marianne Sprangers was born in Wisconsin's udder territory, where beer-cheese soup is a real thing. Free-range, grass fed, and creative, she has earned a couple of unrelated degrees and has been consistent in holding a day job while spending after-work hours in pursuit of her dreams.

Not long ago, Sprangers relocated to North Carolina. It was here where her pen hit the paper and she began an earnest pursuit of actually writing versus just talking about doing it someday. Though the day job modus operandi still holds strong, Sprangers is excited to see where her writing and other creative pursuits will take her next.

www.ingramcontent.com/pod-product-compliance
Lightning Source LLC
Chambersburg PA
CBHW062132040426
42335CB00039B/2078